OUR COMMON SOULS

NEW & SELECTED POEMS OF DETROIT

KEN MEISEL

BLUE HORSE PRESS   REDONDO BEACH, CALIFORNIA   2020

OUR COMMON SOULS

NEW & SELECTED POEMS OF DETROIT

KEN MEISEL

Blue Horse Press

Cover photo by author
Author photo by Keith Meisel

Editors: Jeffrey and Tobi Alfier
Blue Horse Press logo: Amy Lynn Hayes (1996)

ISBN 978-0-578-50867-2

FIRST EDITION © 2020

This and other Blue Horse Press Titles may be found at www.bluehorsepress.com

Ken Meisel writes Detroit, crafting poems of that city's streets and alleys, its bars and monuments, its abandoned factories and landmarks – and most of all, its people. These poems acknowledge familiar long-gone ghosts, like Marvin Gaye, but also those who might otherwise have been forgotten. These poems more often reveal the lives still lived amid the ruins of this city, like the half-ghosts – an abused girl, a junkie, a man begging by the side of the road – who embody the struggles to survive in a place with little hope, as well as the fully engaged who bear witness to how the city's past, to 1967 and factory life and the exhilaration of Detroit music, remains active in its present.

To write about this city is necessarily to write about race – a challenging and essential task that Meisel tackles with care and complexity. In these poems, we hear a psychotherapist's insight into how poverty, vulnerability, pride, and conflict shape racial interactions but also the unavoidable privilege of a straight, white, middle-class man observing Black lives. Some of this is uncomfortable, but even when these poems wrestle with the difficulties of racial tension, they do so with a sense of idealism, always asking how rage intersects with love, how injustice gestures toward possibility.

Meisel's poems are steeped in both popular music and high culture, weaving together references to Motown singers and French artists, Gordon Parks and Plato, demanding that we take the voices and images of Detroit seriously. Flautists playing classical works in the old Michigan terminal building matter as much as here a jazz saxophonist improvising at Baker's Lounge. And all of it is personal as well as communal, seen through the eyes of individuals but located, always, within the still living memory and daily experience of the people of this city.

Ken Meisel's poems take us inside the contemporary social and material landscape of Detroit, rewriting the city's much-documented ruins as entryways to the present as well as the past. These poems remind us that past and present intertwine in relationships – with each other, with the stories that shaped us, in the places where we came from and where we live now.

Sherry Linkon, Professor of English / Director of American Studies, Georgetown University, author of *The Half-Life of Deindustrialization*

"Identity is responsible for the naïve assumption that the psychology of one man is like that of another, that the same motives occur everywhere, that what is agreeable to me must obviously be pleasurable for others, that what I find immoral must also be immoral for them, and so on. Identity, too, forms the basis of suggestion and psychic infection…but identity also makes possible a consciously collective social attitude, which found its highest expression in the Christian ideal of brotherly love."

– C. G. Jung (p 261 Basic Writings)

"Oh let me teach you how to knit again
this scattered corn into one mutual sheaf,
these broken limbs into one body"

– Shakespeare, Titus Andronicus, Act V, Scene iii

Acknowledgments

Poems in this collection have been selected from the previously published books:

Sometimes the Wind (2002): At the Detroit River, January, 1996; Rehearsing at the Fox Theater; 1970; 27 East Willis; Still Life: Sunlight Healing a Brush Park Mansion.

Before Exiting (2006): The Lady Under the Viaduct; Hamtramck; Mr. Rogers in Detroit City.

Just Listening (2007): The Gift of the Gratia Creata; Letter to Kierkegaard; Spring, in Hamtramck; For a Junkie Shooting Up; Tamika's Eyes; Man at Exit 210, I-94, Detroit.

Beautiful Rust (2009): The Archivists of the Incomprehensible; Concrete Art; At the Rinaldo Arms Manor, an Obituary; With My Father & My Great Uncle & the Girl with the Painted Face in the Burnt Out Hotels of Detroit; Detroit City Notebook; Falling Love, 1986; The Lamb Skin Company; He Helps Me Count What's Left Behind; John Lee Hooker's Boogie Chillun; Song of Detroit; Marvin Gaye & the Wrecking Ball; Detroit Meat Warehouse; Diana Ross & The Supremes; Our Common Souls; Elegy for the Residents of the Niagara Apartments; Two Men Watching Martha Reeves & The Vandellas Exit the 20 Grand; Portrait of Miles Davis at the Bluebird Inn, 1953; Elegy for Whatever Isn't Right; Grand River Avenue, Detroit Riots, 1967; The Myth of Fins; The Smell of His Black Skin on My White Skin; Beautiful Rust; Sports; The City is a Woman; Green; Fist; Sculpture.

Scrap Metal Mantra: Poems (2013): St. Catherine of Genoa, at the Rinaldo Arms Manor; Elegy for Deletha; I Want to Tell You; Great Days; The Flautists at the Michigan Central Train Depot; Scrap Metal Mantra; The Burnt Out Prodigals of the Train Station; Scrappers; At the Blue Diamond Lounge; Inamorata; Jesus of the Scrap Yards; Detroit Hymnal; Automotive Wedding, Packard Junkyard, Piquette Avenue; Friday Night in Excelsis (Detroit); At Better Made Potato Chips, Gratiot Avenue, Detroit.

The Drunken Sweetheart at My Door (2015): The Girls at the Vista Maria Home for Truants.

Mortal Lullabies (2018): Watching Bilal Fall.

Many thanks to the following journals, in which some of the new poems in this collection first appeared:

Collateral Damage Anthology: Tamika's Eyes
Concho River Review: 1981, Revisited
Midwestern Gothic: Smoke; Letter from the New Center District; Desultory Refrain for the Packard Plant, Detroit
Muddy River Poetry Review: Sea Gull, on the Delray Bridge
Pea River Journal: Apocalypse Refrain (Detroit)
Peninsula Poets: Letter to Jack Ridl, from Marshall's Bar
Rattle: Art Installation
San Pedro River Review: Letter to J. Alfier, From the Rouge River, at Delray; Letter to Tobi Alfier, From Heidelberg St.; To the Broken Statues in a Field, Detroit; Letter to Terry Blackhawk, from Mt. Hazel Cemetery
Soundings East: The Night My Brother & I Were Bats
The MacGuffin: Watching De'Sean Jones at Baker's Keyboard Lounge
Wayne Literary Review: Cass Avenue Epistle

This book is dedicated to my siblings, Kevin, Kathy, Keith and Kelly ~

27 East Willis is dedicated to Moti Friedler

Elegy for the Residents of the Niagara Apartments is dedicated to Sherry Linkon

Zombieland is dedicated to Keith & Stefani Meisel

The Starlings Over Washington Boulevard is dedicated to Kathy Spencer

The Monumental Classic Cars go to Heaven is dedicated to Todd Gault

1) I credit many of the ideas in the poem *Woodward Avenue Elegy* to the esteemed work of Jerry Herron, from his book, **AfterCulture: Detroit and the Humiliation of History (1993)**

2) The poem *Watching De'Sean Jones at Baker's Keyboard Lounge* was nominated for a Pushcart Prize.

Contents

Detroit River, January, 1996

River on this coal-blasted shore,
River whose name now starts with a fist,
ends on its knees in St. Lawrence,
River whose hands have frozen in prayer,
whose knees sludge through the dark
murky mire; the internecine spaces
where boat hulls and netting embrace,
River whose bottom has no soul, whose
surface bobs with tints of gray steel,
whose throat swallows River Rouge;
River whose mind is void of all memory,
whose jagged fingertips have turned to green ice,
River of sunken beer bottles, churn on.

Rehearsing at the Fox Theater

My father's big band, rehearsing
at the Fox Theater, 1936
crank-up of tenor saxophones
blurp blurp blurp
spank of trumpet arpeggios
through the thick acoustics,
the drummer, smacking sticks
across the dry surface of a snare
like a shotgun in a storm;
the janitor, pausing, to listen:
the trombone section, burping, bellowing,
the piano player, chopping
4/4 time like a choir
thumping on the pews. Snap
of music on the music stands,
Sam Donahue, cuing up
the horn section, the girl singer
crunching out her cigarette,
someone belching up
last night's beer buzz, a
sudden movement up the stairs of sound,
exploding into swing.

1970

At the first listening to Creedence
Clearwater Revival's
      Up Around the Bend,

that song of jagged strangling guitar sounds
screaming through the stereo speakers
      like a rip saw
cutting a big log in half,
      or a speed boat cutting a wake
through a shallow lake,

and John Fogerty yelping out
"there's a place up ahead and we're going"

      my brother and I
stood mute along a stairwell in a kid's basement
      half-drugged in amazement

as his older sister undressed herself,
      to show us her breasts.

The Monumental Parties of 1973
– for John Niemisto

To bring the world to the edge, beyond the Beatles,
        we'd gather together –
                me, Kevin, John, Kathy, Claudia,

sometimes Mark and Paul, Barb, Mary, even Keith,
        and others –
                and we'd huddle together,

sipping the six packs and lighting up someone's
        joint,
                and John, bless him,

would rave on about Jethro Tull, Kraftwerk,
        and bands like Mott The Hoople,
                Humble Pie, Pink Floyd, Sabbath,

or people like David Bowie, Marc Bolan, Alice Cooper,
        Roxy Music, Deep Purple, and, lit up,
                the universe as we knew it,

would burst.
        Every neighborhood needs an oracle,
                a soothsayer, an icon,

someone larger than its side streets implied reach,
        and John, standing at six foot eight,
                a giant, was ours.

I remember the monumental parties of 1973,
        how John held epic court there,
                rolling his generous head back,

laughing into the Universe his musical options.
How he'd grab the new songs
like bolts of audio-fire into his hand.

How he'd hoist them upwards to the summer sky:
like for instance Led Zepplin's
When the Levee Breaks

crashing up through the summer crickets' caesura
where beyond the neighborhood's
Holy Scripture of boys

testing one another out for who would lead
them beyond themselves,
John's hand rose up – again –

his palms full of new music,
like a Goliath so triumphant
in Heavenly reach.

Ideogram: 16205 Westbrook, Detroit's West Side

A home, just a floating video camera where life
      and death,
            feet off the ground in flight,

defined us. The father, his dependable drum set
      packed in the station wagon;
           and the mother — still with us — whose eyes

saw the world annihilated
      when her son died, in December, 1973.
           And the snows blew over us

on black winds larger than stone monuments
      as they tormented us and then
           blew apart every window pane

until something strong and alive was dismembered,
      was blown apart — like time itself —
           and then remembered.

I'm here to tell you of it. Me — hiding in history's curtain —
      whose boy-heart was lit up and flushed
           with summertime fireflies;

and the songs of autumn — so incendiary — inflamed
      the days and the long years
           and then whole decades fell to pieces

across the lonesome sidewalks
      and they were remembered again
           by the seasons. Me, this reporter

of a family's history
      written inside a set of missing words
           we've stopped listening

to anyway – these hushed words
        about seven people in a family –
            offered here for you

about how a middle child died inside our midst,
        here at this home address, this ideogram
            right here, right now…

Just an ideogram commemorating a boy's death
        right there on a hospital bed.
            Gone, like a leaf from a small tree.

Gone because the tree – it seems – didn't want
        him hanging around it. Just a little leaf
            tossed off limb to roam the wind.

And my youngest brother – hiding – stumbled upon
        by his older sister as he sat so hollowed-out
            in the early January snow fall's mist:

battling the howling absence of his dead brother after he'd ran –
        against time – around the whole block;
            his interior monologue

something none of us knew; and my sister, holding him;
        and me, just a boy in the absence,
            in the empty grave, grieving the dead brother

and seeking himself in the *other*, in the identical twin,
        and the both of us, curled tight against
            the loss, the calamitous ruin –

and listening to songs like *Five Years, Idiot Wind,*
        Helter Skelter, Monkey Man,
            just to find dislocation's prophet.

The rest of me, so silent as I wandered,
        walked the cement wall past the church,

7

pondering the fiery words

of St. John of the Apocalypse, and why it was a person, *me*,
            would have the ears left to hear
                  what had been left so unsaid —

just to recall it all and then, write it all out later —
            when the mystery of its true meaning
                  could find me, an onlooker, a witness.

Me, who'd have to chase
            a younger brother's vanishing footsteps
                  beyond an inhospitable tree

that had chucked him,
            like a small vibrant leaf, away. Right into death.
                  I'd shuffle through

a pickpocket pile of other leaves,
            just a musty scattered orphanage that,
                  already roughly dispersed,

would, like a poacher's attendant,
            steal one more vital leaf for its dismal pile…
                  And then, I'd find *me*, running alone

down the hillside of a small city park,
            searching for that one flung, brilliant bursting leaf —
                  pitched from a tree's limb

onto a pile of other cheerless autumn-colored orphaned leaves
            that had been blown,
                  flung out, forsaken…me, looking for my brother.

I could never find him under the leaves.
            Would hear his voice in the brittle wind.
                  Would feel him rushing past me.

I'd then convince myself my lips kept secrets,

my mouth, to rest in quietude
as I counted the long days

until we all left that house so loud with anguish
and so dense with words of love,
crushed down to silence.

I'd sit alone, there in the park, spellbound,
trying to find the leaf. Would get up, run,
carry in my possessed heart

the sound of his voice that we'd all hold tight
to ourselves and share, still later,
speaking in tongues against the gravity

of death's possessor. And me: I'd be waiting, hesitating,
captivated by the torment
that penetrated all the darkness. I'd be

filled up too, with the absence and the presence
of that home – 16205 Westbrook –
as we finally walked away from it,

as we closed the door behind it to leave it forever –
the new day, breaking warm behind us…
the July humidity engulfing us

as we wiped the hot sweat from our foreheads
on the next morning…
And me, I stood solitary there –

looking into it: that house, that childhood
home, so enigmatic – this house,
this home – this ideogram of self

that had forced me to contend with my grief –
because a lonesome leaf had gone flying away from me,
like a slipped after-thought.

Yesterday, alone, I looked at it again:
        I stood in front of it, alone, free.
                It was treasure not stumbled

upon but, in fact, it was a resurrection zone
        where I was born
                and where I did die

in a property of blood and fraternity,
        in a patriarchy and a matriarchy,
                and in a property of death

where the second coming is a fulfillment
        of the first,
                from this home, this hearth,

from this ideogram of self where I was
        to fruitlessly pursue a leaf, a kid brother
                as he frolicked away

from me into vacuity, into futility,
        and into a vast nothingness
                like a vial of celestial light

moving farther and farther away from me –
        so that I'd have to chase him
                until he entranced me,

he plagued, taunted and he mesmerized me
        and he rendered me a fugitive
                to myself –

so that I'd then be tempted to chase him
        again and again, until he
                then defeated me,

this younger brother who died
        in a hospital room like a white leaf
                in a lonesome leaf pile,

and he humbled me too, so that I'd leave him be –
    this boy, this bright faultless leaf
        I so loved there, now dead.

One night my brother spoke to me.
    He told me to run away from me.
        He told me that

the static pose and the vivid current
    of all things we believe in
        are nothing like we guess. Told me

that the heart of a bursting atom
    is where the light of all dying things
        divine themselves. Told me

to rest my thoughts in celebration
    instead of remorse,
        and then he told me

that this house – at 16205 Westbrook
    on Detroit's West Side –
        was a resurrection zone

where I was then reborn healed,
    before and then after
        my torment, again.

27 East Willis

Here is the place where I saved a dog's life
as it lunged forward, paw-over-step into the bustling
city traffic on a cold January morning;
and the sewer grates blew white steam seven feat high
into the cold morning air. And to love a world
slowly dying before your eyes, you had to save something
from its perishing just once. Here is the place
where I almost strangled a black boy's neck with my bare
hands because he was walking down the road
with a yellow-handled screwdriver, keying
the side doors of every parked car. And when I
let go of his shirt he ran away like a scared antelope,
and I worried for his future and mine. Here is the place
where I rushed into my living room
and saw my room ransacked, my clothes strewn
all over, and my money spilled on the bed,
and the rear door of my apartment hanging open
like a mouth in the wind, the sound of a kid's feet
running away. Here is the place where I stood
with a cup of hot coffee at the edge of Woodward in 1983,
and watched the Thanksgiving Day parade
marching by me. Watched a couple of Michael Jacksons
prancing and dancing white-gloved across
the pavement, and Madonna-wanna-bes
flirting and dancing between Snow White and Popeye,
and even Santa Claus at the back of the pack.
Here is the place where I took a warm bath in a big tub
with a woman who'd become my wife,
and the hair on my arms shimmered like white fleece
as I rubbed soap on her body; and I offered
her wine. And the city outside raged with sirens
and angry voices that crumbled like salt. Here is the place

where my neighbor who was a plumber and a loner
died in his sleep like a large piece of wood graying to stone,
and the police hauled him out on a stretcher
while everyone huddled and looked. And the Asian
woman who lived down the hall pounded the piano
that evening, threatening God with the *Moonlight Sonata.*
Here is the place where my brother threw away
a portrait of himself as a housewife washing dishes
in a pair of yellow gloves. And the redheaded landlady
leaned her generous face through my doorway
like a white-faced ghost, drunk, and she kissed me.
And then she struggled back down the hallway
running a finger down the crumbling plaster and tile.
Here is the place where the whores and junkies
sometimes froze on the fences in a stupor,
and you'd read about them the next frigid morning
fixed in their death-trance like bronze statues.
Here is the place where rats scurried along two-by-fours
inside my walls, and German cockroaches
scattered under my slippers like pieces of peanut-brittle.
Here is the place where late at night I listened to Keith Jarrett's
The Koln Concert and I imagined my living room
was an arena filled with the sentient creatures of Heaven.
And the soft summer breezes, wafting the machinery
of Detroit through my window, sometimes glowed,
as if filled with hordes of lightning bugs or faint stars
of fragments of deep music or literature or grief.
And I prayed on my knees for the strength to live
through the next morning without surrendering to self-pity,
or to the Seven Deadly Sins lurking like ghosts.
And Van Morrison's *Into the Mystic* lifted me
from the shell of my body like an astral rhythm,
lifted me up like a crazy little tugboat reaching
backward to catch me from my drowning, or my swerving,
into that green envy of never having enough.

Still Life: Sunlight Healing
A Brush Park Mansion

Look: The morning sunlight is a blessing, penetrating
the hollow vacancy of a ruined mansion,
the fallen lord of a pockmarked, desolate street.
One among the many that have been abandoned,
left to become a tragic pedigree of the 1920's.
Pigeons are spreading on the roof like feathered knights,
and crows, the enemy, are perched in the trees,
cawing out battle songs and general irritation
at the lonesome silence of this dead neighborhood.
The front yard is littered with mansard tiles
and kick molding, and scroll-shaped corbels curling
up in the crabgrass, like white plaster snails.
Who says the sunlight lacks intentionality?
Who says I didn't want to stand here and become
bleached by its altruism? Who says, but this
is just for me. To witness the pattern of sunlight
soothing all that's now wretched and rotten.
Look, the sun swims over the toppled interior walls.
Look, it roams over the punctured dining room floor.
Look, it softly bathes the wounded, collapsed
octagonal roof, now residing in the living room.
And the sun ripples like a stream of holy water
over the side porch. Grape vines are climbing it.
And the two-tiered portico is stained with red lichens
and moss. And out here, amidst the tall vines
that are draping and grasping this old home
for the earth, stealing and possessing it like a band
of wood nymphs, hungry and rotting with the musty
smells of decay – the sunlight sheds luminous,
diaphanous light rays all over the anguish of this
damned house. As if healing it.

The Lady Under the Viaduct

She often cursed out loud for angels,
I'd hear her shouting there as I ran past.
She yelled, commanded, screamed for them,
as if a voice, loud and strident, could
find the angel asleep on the bough of a tree,
deep in the seepage of shrubs and dew,
there in the soft light and glade of bird songs,
owl calls, endless invisible drippings;
and deep in the expanse of an open field
growing outside the cardboard box
she made a salty, rain-drenched home in,
beneath the harsh smokestacks of a factory.
And she was one of the homeless. She was
ravaged, smeared with dirt, with sweat, anger,
for she was bereft of angels, had none.
She'd walk her hours alone, as if born without
a name. She had no guardian angel. She had
nothing resembling the gossamer and linen
of wings that lifted angels beyond the flesh
of human form, for she was bereft of adolescent
turmoil; had none of the infinitesimal
longings that angels bring with them to us
as fits of melancholy, as bittersweetness, reverie,
for she was plainly angry to be without them,
angels. And she yelled again and again
at the bridge, and at trucks passing above her
on the noisy overpass – where a murky river
moved nothing but grease and production
forward from a steel plant. And in her rage,
she'd yell that an angel lived in the chimneys.
And she called it mercy, she called it monster.
She called it mother.

Hamtramck

Once I was up late, in December.
I was twenty two. It was snowing,
and the dark trees were slowly
filling up with snow and moisture
so that if you looked deep
enough into them, by God you'd see
that they were glistening.
This was in the city of Hamtramck,
and I was outside, listening
to the night. I saw a woman, she
was foreign, I think from the Ukraine,
and she was quietly weeping,
holding her face in a blue towel.
It was Christmas, and the decorative
lights were draped like garland
across the snowy bushes and roofs.
Some bulbs were blue, some red,
some green, and some of the lights,
wrapped tightly around tree trunks,
shined opaque. There had been
a harsh quarrel, a fight, between a man
and a woman, I think this woman
weeping nearby, and then, silence.
The night had absorbed everything.
And the cars lumbered sluggishly
over the white, snow-covered streets.
Slowly, the evening lights darkened
and all I could hear were the sounds
of salt trucks chugging down roads,
and the grunts and the heavy stepping
of bruised men, leaving the bars.
Someone had said that Santa Claus
would sail over the Davison Freeway,
and he would tug hard on the ropes,
urging the reindeer toward Grosse Pointe,

by passing Hamtramck all together,
because no one was joyous here.
Not the hard lucked, shell-faced laborers.
Not the broken-hearted women.
Not even the dirty-faced children.
I wanted to step through the light snow.
Touch this woman on her shoulder,
comfort her, because she was weeping.
I was twenty two and very alone.
I didn't have the language to soothe
anyone yet. And even if I did, it still
may not have mattered, nor done any good.
The night was as silver as Heaven.
The trees held all of the secrets about
loving a person I didn't yet know.
The woman groaned from her throat.
I hid behind a railing, watching her.

Mr. Rogers in Detroit City

It's a wonderful day in the neighborhood
mumbles Mr. Rogers,
sifting through an overflowing trash can
back, behind my apartment building,
where the tomcats, fed on discarded
tuna cans and headless fish guts
and chicken parts from the Eastern Market
chase big rats, and glass bottles
are hurled at them for sport late at night,
and still later, at 3am, for all of us
to hear, two grown men working
through the delirium tremens, fist fight
over the absurd gladiator contest
of whose grocery cart, filled to the top
with returnable bottles, got to the shady spot first,
under the haggard old maple tree
in front of the building where I live –
in order to wait out the thunderstorm,
pelting the streets silver-blue.
It's a wonderful day up on Martin Luther
King Boulevard where the crack addicts
who were once school girls counting
the days to their first kiss, are now counting
the cash received after quick sex
at a motel. And Rogers, moving past there,
hums to himself what a wonderful world
this is, here, where a lady grins at him
from a stoop, her front teeth full of flowers
and her laughing eyes quinine-stained,
and up on a window ledge, overlooking the street,

a whole row of red geraniums equals art.
It's a wonderful day up on Cass Avenue
where the junkies are lined up like emaciated
zombies outside the blood bank
for a donation and $10. It's a wonderful day
in the neighborhood
back behind the old Vernor's Plant
where a dog's been barking for five days
and chasing a wild pheasant
through glass debris. It's a wonderful
day in the neighborhood
mumbles Mr. Rogers on his way past the half-
way house on East Willis,
and the crazies who live there spit
and drool, but there's an old black lady there
who's smile outlasts the sunset,
and he stops there for a visit with her,
and the tired afternoon, hot and lazy
and tinted olive-yellow by car exhaust,
wilts, and it burns out like a cigar.
And dusk equals the collapse of men
under the shady trees past Second Avenue,
some drunk, some junked-up on smack,
but that's not all – it also equals
hissing window fans, and men smashing bottles
in the alleyways. And police sirens
squealing like a bad temper from the precinct
on Woodward. And dusk also equals the sunset
shimmering over the Ren Cen downtown
where the cross-way streets are together being burned,
for there's blood too, and more
contention outside the New Miami
which has been boarded up for months
where two men fight over there, from the mad rage
of being homeless and filthy, and

without a woman to hold them up or hoist
them up for their dignity; and Rogers,
strolling past them, is inflamed with awe,
like a torched person, an idiot savant.
It's a wonderful day in the neighborhood
and Roger's bum leg aches outside
a party store, up on Trumbull, where the
Wayne State University football team
practices drills, and the bright-faced young
cheerleaders kick the air and twist-and-spin
like Musketeers, and the linden trees,
yellowed and withered now, are dropping
their leaves like hankies. And autumn,
which is the rough equivalent of a festival
of delight and leprosy, is not quite yet
the color of blood and gasoline
here on the street where the 67' riots sizzled,
but close. And Rogers, wearing a Tigers cap, sings
the soul-breaking song of the desolation of angels
wilting like flowers alongside a fence,
and then he mutters, and then he finally laughs.

The Gift of the "Gratia Creata"

— Hamtramck, MI

To know the truth, in this city,
a man's vacant eyes say to me on the street,
— his mouth frothing with liquor
and the spit of too many old wounds —
is to know pain and drunkenness,
public displays of dirty emotion,
joblessness and a lasting humiliation.
Fights that last forty minutes
over a married woman. Or someone
walking too close to someone else.
It's just an innuendo full of blue flame.
Someone's black boots stepping
too hard over someone's shoe heel,
and all those liquor shots consumed,
never mind the religion on Sunday.

          All the same,
it's what matters
most to those who stumble below me
to get it right each time they do it,
to follow this broken dance into oblivion,
and so the sidewalk below is full.
And so are the bars along the street.
I'm in an open window gazing
at the road full of cars. The night air
is full of aromas, pierogi, kielbasa,
stench of vomit, car fume exhaust.

There is a trombone, my father's
that we keep here at the window.
It's for the offertory. We blow it loud
when the drunks get too unholy,
and the full moon fails to calm them
down or still them. When their
sad wives with faces of spilled milk,
and eyes turned to suspicious
red flames wait for them underneath
the covers, and nothing else changes
for them night to night.

                                There is
a song too, but the women shush it
on their lips with fingers dusted with
flour. It is the song of the *gratia
creata*, the divine love and its work —
that blessing that "fills the bread
of the soul" in another with grace,
that "stirs a foul man past his nature."
An old woman in a babushka says
this to me with a fierce conviction,
her little eyes blazing with holy fire,
though the street knows nothing of it,
nor do the priests who buy bread —
for it's a gift from the holy guilds
of the bakery, here in the midst of town.
It's "the secret" she wants me to know.
It's a prayer whipped and it's leavened
with a woman's two callused palms,
with the bruised lips of her faith.
It's for the dead men they go on loving,
those, drinking themselves into death.
It's sung hard, into the fresh bakery bread.

Man at Exit 210, I-94, Detroit

You are the one at the edge
of the road with the frown
of your two eyes lifted in your hands
seeking someone's handouts,
as if they are gold. You are the
rose at the edge of the road,
withered by drought. You are the
man asking for nothing,
because there is nothing left
of your life but what you are
asking for,
which is something between
mercy and loose change.
And when a man begs another
for loose change, it is because
one life is bleeding into another
life, and there's no way to
escape it or run from it,
because it seeps like a bad debt
into the memory,
and so I am a part of your
keeping today. I am your keeper.
Daumier, the artist, understood how it is
your face became this twisted
figure eight turned psychotic.
He understood how poverty
corrupts the smile, makes it
grimace like the moon over a swamp.
Of course Goya also knew
what happens when the Devil,
which is God's evil twin,
corrupts the body into its

incandescent filtering of light.
The horror — and how it
cascades through the bones,
turns a man into wax.
Sometime, before you became
this aspect of God's poverty,
this completed gesture of one
life shamelessly lived on a corner,
you were the child pushed
by the stroke of God's hand
down a stairwell, into your
destiny. You were the light
of the birth room, and some-
body lifted you high, whispered
this riddle into your ear,
this riddle that would carry
you to your soul's making,
to the stroke and kick
of becoming a man on a corner,
broken in two like Pinocchio,
shattered like a glass globe
into charcoal fragments,
and seeking my extra change.
Your face is black hole.
Daumier understood that one too,
because a face covered in ash
is a face void of the lantern
that keeps us crawling up
from the hidden cave
into something like enlightenment,
which Plato understood
as the dark ground of our being,
and which you understand,
no doubt, as just the filth
of wearing the same tattered shirt,

and living one coin at a time.
Every day that I drive past you,
I hear the music in your ears.
It is the song of the whip-
poorwill throttled alive
in the underbrush. It is the song
of God, asking to see my mercy.
It is the song of the social
conscience, which neither cares
nor doesn't care, but just
does what it does to get by,
as if dealing the cards
in a deck on the way to the ace.
You are the song of extinction.
Beating one car at a time.

For a Junkie Shooting Up

Once, when there was nothing
left in the sky but big clouds,
and a rainfall that was just starting
to spit, I saw a woman shooting
up, scoring before nightfall,
in the rough edge of a field
where there used to be a building.
She was part animal now,
and part orphan, as if she'd once
belonged to somebody, but not
any more. Now she belonged to
whatever it is takes a body out,
past the spotlight of common
sense and decency, and into
whatever it is becomes of somebody
seeping like backwash, away.
If you were a novelist, you'd
note in the scene that a person
committing suicide by injection
refuses to acknowledge her
creator, you, and so you'd feel
the guttural emptiness that addiction
or loneliness always brings.
If you were a pulp fiction writer
you'd give her a black eye,
and a backside of scars. And a pimp
lurking behind her like charcoal.
And if you were a talking head
you'd discuss socio-economic
reasons for why it is she's frothing
at the mouth and bleeding
for the sake of societal problems,

and for opportunities dried up.
If you were a painter brushing
this scene into truthfulness,
you'd add the white ghosting
of malevolent death stalking
her like a cloudy shadow. And if you
were Gordon Parks, the photographer,
you'd paste in a picture
of her anguished grandmother,
tears like streams of mercury
rolling down her dark crinkled face.
The five year old daughter
peering bashfully at the camera,
another child of the State.
And if you were Chirico, you'd see
there was a dog, too. It roamed
uneasily past the corner party
store and down, beyond the
apartment buildings, as if searching
for somebody lost. If you were
a poet describing what you saw,
you'd invent a word for people
being consumed by leprosy
of the soul. It would have to rhyme
with awe but not belong
to God or the Devil, but rather
to the negotiation in between light
and sadness, where the beings
who've not yet decided who they
belong to, truly live. Not ghosts,
you'd have to point out,
so much as those in between
ghosts and the living forgetables.
Those that wild dogs smell.
Long before the morning comes.

Letter To Kierkegaard

"Oh, the sins of passion and of the heart,
how much nearer to salvation than the
sins of reason!"
        —Kierkegaard

                         Soren,
the world is a sickness unto death,
smoke stacks refusing God
or leaps of faith – in fact,
the snow in Detroit is as dreadful
as where you wrote Regina love letters.
Even if your words about trying
to oppose intelligence *don't* live on,
they've succeeded, here in Detroit,
where nobody reads poems that grieve
for our lungs being riddled with
carbon-monoxide.
All the same, the hotel where I write
this has brass door knobs
and maid service, even though
the curtains are ripped
and the windows overlook an iron
river spilling into waste basins,
and there's a salvage yard collecting
metal parts.
Soren, nobody, not even you, said
we have to collect junk to learn
who we are. If you had faith, you
would have stayed with Regina,
and I wouldn't have pissed Anita off
either. Faith is the heart's needle
of the bereft. And that's a maxim
we both believe in, because we are
philosophers of either/or; we're
as divided down the middle as this
room splits in half, two beds apiece.
Soren, I hear echoes laughing

down the grim yellow hallways
where one light bulb per every ten feet
scolds us. And I smell the after-
burn of lovers screwing hard
and fighting even harder as dusk
pelts the river with ashes.
You know yourself that the dreadful
sickness of cities pulverizing
themselves to smoke holds no promise
for love or involvement.
Sickness is sinfulness, you said,
you muttered it really, pushing past
those street urchins in Copenhagen,
those that laughed.
I can taste that bitterness, rising
in my throat like somebody's fist.
I can smell that laughter that humiliates,
even when it's my own.
You'll arrive by plane tomorrow
with a brief case of poetry for Regina.
That's good that you're trying poems.
Philosophy won't win her back,
too many ideas that amount to intell-
igence masturbating. I don't mean
any offense. You know despair's so
personal. I know it too, I've just ordered
a cheap plate of fries
and the sirens outside don't bring
her any closer to me.
I'm not drinking, Soren, and I hope
you're not either. Liquor is no answer
for hope feeling hungry for prayer.
I'm lucky if I can get one love poem
off to her. Send it by morning mail.
And nothing in your heart or mine
is like ordering food alone in a hotel
trying hard not to rot from the foundation

up — it won't get either of us closer to
God, or to the delicate bones in a woman's
face we're both missing, skin-to-skin.
Heartbreak's the first sign
of sinfulness rotting from the inside
out. Then, fear and trembling,
melancholy, despair, intellectual
arrogance, spite and sickness —
each one of these moods you've held
in your palm. Me too, though the sun,
evaporating into pollution over
the Detroit River seeks no solution,
nothing in your books nor mine;
nothing of mercy, nothing of God's hand,
nothing of the loss of the eternal,
other than the dusk.

Tamika's Eyes

Tamika's just fourteen and she's been raped
on a cardboard box by a man in an alleyway,
under a sprawling maple tree that's gone yellow.
This is in Detroit, where random acts of violence,
mixed into the high clouds with a factory smog
slithering across the sky in filthy rain squalls,
marks all our days. And grief – which is the
way that the eyes catalogue pain – comes forth
in big spools of tears and woe.

Tamika tells me the story as we play crazy eight's.
It's strange, a girl of fourteen telling me a man's
sins back to me. Especially when she still
paints her finger nails pink and sleeps curled up
with a teddy bear in her bed. A girl shouldn't
have to tell a man's sins back to him,
but she tells me, and so I'm a part of her story.

This is also the year I learn that pain is contagious.
And, because I am still young, and I don't yet
know that pain is contagious and it disables
a part of you forever if you take it,
I take it from a girl telling me a man's story
back to me, and it disables me, and that's
why I am like this now. I have some of a girl's
damage inside of me. You know, it's as if I, too,
am infected with a part of this girl's life.
It's as if I, too, am blessed with this kind of luck.

I tell you, when Tamika cries, it's astonishing
what her face does, for she cries deeply,
like a kid in a mirror trying to find herself
from some sort of erasing that has happened to her.
Sometimes she cries herself into breathlessness,
and she has to grab her shoulders and slow down.
And her grief resembles a child awakening
from some kind of nightmare because it is wide-eyed
and astonished. It's full of her eye's heartbreak.

And when I look at how she cries, it's like she's
breaking the bloodied peat moss of her heart
across her own two hands — as an act of anguish
and sorrow against a violent event that's happened
to her little body, which is the only definition
of war I can think of that everyone *believes*,
because the body is the sacred symbol of the world
being torn asunder or cradled in safety…

~

I suppose it's true that a girl sized up by somebody
with a prize on his mind is a girl marked,
and what is left of the stars in her back pocket
that you think she ought to reach for,
well, they really amount to something as small
as crushed dollar store beads. And the little lamps
that are her eyes trying to see a world's
character flaws, or its snows of spring flowers
rising simultaneously together,
stay fixed in bewilderment forever, or else
she gouges out their future light
with the nervous tips of her fingers in the after-flow
of trauma and shame and self-woe,
and she's left blinded, just like a stunned angel,
she's a rabbit in the middle of a road
trying to crawl back to where things started.

But Tamika tells me she's glad we cried together.
She says, sometimes, all we can do is open
our eyes and cry, until all the hurt in there is gone.
And then she sits back, heaves a big round sigh.
And the noises of the city enter the room again.
We hold hands in silence, like old friends.

I figure we're all like conduits that conduct
each other's pain no matter what the casualties are,
no matter what the gains and losses will be...
Maybe that's why beauty and evil come together,
and the shared sexes have to deal with it.
And if we don't conduct it, I guess we're both just
lost, and either way we're both together,
either way we both carry the burden, and it stains
the one big quilt that is our shared life,
and that is the law of contagion that makes us.

~

When Tamika first sees me, she's at the top
of the stairway ready for bed, her teddy bear
tucked under her elbow. Her eyes are like steel...
Her fingers twirl a sharp yellow pencil,
as if she's waiting for one more man to attack.
When I say goodbye to Tamika for the last time
she tells me I'm like her uncle, even though
I'm white. Her eyes, though they're full of mist,
shine like she's trying to find Heaven,
and she tells me she hopes she can get
herself back to into school, in one safe piece.
It's as if she's ghosted in a mirror –
like she's waiting for something to get clear –
and if she is to find herself again in a man's eyes,
and see herself better, she must find
someone to tell it to, and this time it was me.

Spring, in Hamtramck

I remember it as a brightness
without personality, a fever,
a pilgrimage of heated light
spreading across the crusty
snow like a blessing from above,
coloring the whole street yellow.
And from my window, over-
looking the beat-up avenue,
overlooking the rows of junked cars,
overlooking the scrofulous
row houses made of asbestos,
their roofs, ruined, their
porches sprained and soaked,
their front lots, drained,
made of the broken-down dreams
of laborers living their hard-
scrabble lives – some of them
losing themselves in their nightly
addictions, some, in their daily
assassinations of themselves,
some, getting lost in their children,
or in their wives with their grim,
somnambulant eyes – all of them
wishing for some hope of a grand
future more promising than this one,
the morning moved like a stream
of sunlight, touching the snowy lawns
and baptizing light into
the nakedness of the dormant bushes,
into the stiffness of trees,
and I remember how blessed
we all felt, how suddenly alive. . .

And I remember a woman, a
mother so beautiful you could
see what cruelty would do to her,
to the smooth skin of her face,
how it would turn the heart
in her body into a wilted flower,
a smashed, shriveled lump
at the mercy of an angry man,
or an angry world that'd taken her.
She was standing, arms open,
there with her young son
holding onto his hand. They
were gazing at the spring sunshine
dappling the streets with light
and shadow. It was flooding
the condemned lots and twirling
halos around the tall steeples.
She was gesturing to him,
arms open, shoulders spread
so wide that anyone could see
her blue nightgown, her bosom,
her cleavage like a meadow,
her heart like a violet opening
itself up to the first sunlight.
She told him to open his arms,
like her, to springtime's fever.
I could see how the pain of living
in that city so full of ruined lives
could fulfill all it is we take
to us as blind devotion, as a desire
to love what it is we can't ever
carry – those sins of husbands
who've been broken, or have been
strangled to a strict compromise
by the wintering over of the

heart as it turns to closed gears —
men, whose hearts are closed fists.
And their ruddy cheeks, bloody,
their muscles like armor. . .
I watched from my window
what it was she was doing:
her arms were moving tentacles.
Her eyes were like flowers.
Her mouth like a flowing river.
How it was she was showing him
a glimpse of her inner world:
that to make love with some-
thing is to say *yes*, over
and over again until you are
alive with it. Till it is in you,
forever.

Detroit Meat Warehouse

Underneath the springtime rain
that's moistening the whole sky
with drifting smoke from a wet
mottled fire somewhere over
the factory district, north of here,
and on East Kirby at the corner
of Riopelle amidst filthy refuse
and blown out tires and rusted rims
and somebody's spilled garbage bags…
sits the Detroit Meat Warehouse,
a brick, coral-colored, graffiti stained
building sitting guiltily across the street
from the abandoned Tamaren Beef
Company, and the H&R Packing
Company, both gone to wet smoke
and weeds. I stand outside my car,
sipping on a large coke and munching
on a burger while I read the sign.
It advertises "prime young turkeys,
tender and juicy. Mountain oysters,
hog maws, extra large. And fresh
chitterlings" which are, I should say
pig intestines gathered in a bucket,
boiled, and stinking, and consumed
with yellow mustard in autumn –
by old black men sitting on box crates
and playing cards, and drinking 40 ounce
beers, while the sea gulls swoop
and dive over the refuse, in Detroit.

Concrete Art

– for Kevin, of course

Driving south down Woodward
we'd see the concrete art,
my brother and I, when he
was in art school studying
fine arts, down in the ghetto
of the Cass Corridor, where
the Victorian homes were
collapsing into an eye sore
of demolition, and into shelters
for toothless recovering addicts
and Jackson prison releases.
And after a cup of coffee
at his studio, we'd climb into
his rotting 64' Falcon and
we'd steer off of John R
onto the freeway, and he'd
select and point out the fine art
somehow etched into being
across the overpasses. *Look*,
he'd say, there's a Mark Rothko,
a block of black paint
spread across a concrete face,
and a rectangle of metallic red
probably streaked across
by the state's highway repair crews,
and rising up like a horizon,
suggesting a greater fortune
beyond this tired, industrial
grid of ball bearings and factory life.
Or there's a Robert Motherwell,
a lost frame from the famous

Elegy to the Spanish Republic
Series, black stripes and ovals
crawling across a demolished wall,
highlighting the desperation
and anguish the citizens felt
after the Fascists executed Lorca.
Or he'd point to a crumbling
overpass and identify a
Clifford Still, saying look at
the crawl of paint leaving
blank spots and streaks. As if
the artist, who would have been
the harsh midwest climate,
had ignored the cruel process
of cissing. And had spun away
into another location, leaving
this wind and rain, and the coarse
haphazard city winds to complete
the rest of the job. Or he'd find
a smashed ball of yellow paint
exploded with gusto over a rusty
brown viaduct. And he'd say,
look, there's an Adolph Gottlieb,
Counterpoise circa 1959, one
of the famous pictographs. Put
there by an artist for the people,
signifying ancient hope or peace.
We'd drive on like this. Seeking
evidence there could be something
greater to the demolished cement
of the city's bridges and puddles.
For we were looking for proof
of life amidst this beautiful rust.
For something worth our loving,
here in the ruin.

The Lamb Skin Company
– Detroit's Eastern Market District

Down the street called Adelaide at Orleans Street
you can smell the wet, wounded red stink
   of animals, sheep and steer, and chickens
being slaughtered at the Albadr Slaughter House.
   And, wandering past there, past
pigeons and doves – gilded filthy things prancing
and marching toe underfoot, like irritated
   little emperors stomping through old lettuce –
you arrive, as if by accident or by fate,
at the Lamb Skin Company on Alfred Street,
   across from the older, red bricked slaughter
house that's vacant now, and impregnated
   with garbage both putrid and wet
with last evening's rainfall. And, out of curiosity,
you step across graveled cement into the Lamb
Skin Company. And you find a white woman
   smoking a cigarette and watching a small TV set
   on a stool stained with sweat and grease,
with Rafael, who's the boss here. He tells you
   he's in charge of the sheep skins.
Those leftovers speckled with bugs and tangles
   of gnatted fur and green entrail stains.
And that he trims them and salts them and he
   cares for them as if they're the skins
of old lovers now killed, by hatchets.
And he and I step through the dark dungeon
   of that old building, its ceiling held up
by a stack of wooden, salt grizzled pallets,
and its floor, wet anyhow, with bloodied grit
   and dark salt. All around us skins
are stacked in sloppy piles, like dead coats.
And he tells me, with eyes staring right through
   me, like they're partially blind to humanity,
that a man from China or Turkey,
with an accent silk and oily, will come to him

like a thief in the motor city night.
And he will pull out a wallet, page through money,
and transact a deal for these skins.

With My Father & My Great Uncle
& the Girl with the Painted Face
in the Burnt-Out Hotels of Detroit

Who still lives in the burnt hotels of Detroit? The bricks falling
to pieces and the lost windows like gouged out eyes looking stiffly
at nothing. I once stepped through an old lobby where the wood
railing was rotted down to moisture and ashes, and the marble
flooring was gone, and all that was left was an echo, a few stupid
pigeons on a couch. Old hotels resemble a lost room of memory.
What's in them is sadness. It's burned out like dead perfume.
There's suicide notes, broken tiles, cracked glass mirrors
and steam irons, and sooty lipstick containers, and all the burnt
anguish you feel when you're tired and homesick.

What makes us walk here together, my father, my great uncle and I?
Except for a few drifters, riffling through a duffel bag left on
the street on a Tuesday in late December, nothing is left here
on the road except dirt and black snow. They're at it, the men
in disheveled wet clothing outside of the *2500 Club Sports Bar*, long
vacated of liquor and men on the estranged corner of Henry
and Park, here in Detroit, and one of them, if he's not careful,
is going to pay, that is, if he grabs at it too fast.

You're walking past them and you see one of them pull out a dark shirt,
wrestle with it over his dirty head, get it over himself like
a bad dream. He's planning on his warmth tonight. He'll wrestle with
danger in his cot, north of here at the Rescue Mission,
and someone will try to spit in his soup. It reminds you
of the tangle of sadness, how it's rough going, like a dream. I think I
was once one of them, a resident living at the American Hotel
on Temple & Cass, a junkie. Someone possessed by his own self
revulsion and addiction, and breaking his heart over a filthy sink.

If it wasn't me, then it must've been my late father, a brass horn
under his left arm and sipping a brandy in the Addison Hotel lobby.
If it wasn't my father, worrying himself into melancholy because his
life wasn't even his own, it must've been my great uncle, a stage
actor, shooting heroin into his left arm so as to preserve his right
one, the outgoing one, for waving to fans.

He would've torn his only coat, an old top coat with a brick red
scarf, and pissed his coffee out, back, behind the Charlotte Lounge
where he would've put one on for the ages, like an Irish Hamlet,
and where he would've argued with the wind just like it was his
worried, 'set upon' mother. And he would've paraded out of here
looking for sadness and nothing blowing in the wind between the
stars and the flame-singed hotels, bewitched with his loneliness,
because his desire was dead as a flower, and because Irish sadness
is a tangled dream.

The sewer steam would have dressed him in its stinky gray silk.
And he would've taken a lover, a girl as broken as a dark pipe
and living hand to mouth, a welfare person in the Temple Hotel.
And we would've sung our songs too, he and I and my late father,
and that girl with the painted face and the dark lips, before the
ending robbed us of our shirt collars and our fine ink pens,
and all our voices turned to rust.

The Smell of His Black Skin on My White Skin

What do I make of that boy whose name was Dwayne
and whose bright young grinning face was black as leather
and whose fast young fists were quick as diamonds
when he punched at invisible witnesses to his prowess,
and who, all those years ago at Redford High School
in Detroit, came up shoving on me because he wanted
my girlfriend for himself? What do you say to something
as bold as that? Well, he was bussed into the school
from his own home turf without any vote. And my girlfriend,
who was a cheerleader, and who was on the Homecoming
Court, wore her blond hair just like Farrah Fawcett did,
because it was the style in 1976, so anybody you know
would've desired her, and so he did too. And when he and I
fell into the blending of our colors on a stairwell that led down
to the swimming pool, we were holding onto each other's
shirt collars and threatening to tear the color off each other's
face. Can you believe it, that we would threaten to do that?
He was first to challenge. But I was smaller and afraid
so I got dirty with him and called him nigger which made
him swallow his laughter at me and shove his fist up
my ribs. No one could see us there, engaged in the see-saw
of our combat for a girl. The stairs were near dark because
one of the light bulbs had been punched out by a basketball
player going down to the pool. And so all I could make out
were the snowballs of his two eyes glistening across at me.
And the piano keys of his teeth too as he grinned and taunted me
because I was shaking in my belly and he could feel it, because my
stomach was up against his. Can you imagine the intimacy of such a
scene? And so he pushed me against the old tile wall of the stairwell.
And he challenged me to tear it off – his face that is – the color of it,
because I hated it so much. And I pushed him back against the
opposite wall, sneering at him that if I did it he could just as quickly
tear my color off too, which would make us equal, something like
brothers. Skinless worms entangled, strangling or loving one another.
And he moved his finger and thumb around my neck like he was
going to go ahead and pop the cork off a bottle. And said to me,

admit it, you like colored girls. Which I did. But I was too ashamed to admit it to anyone. And he said, cause I like your white girl, and I wanna feel the white skin up her legs and thighs the way you do – which made me shove him back again, up into the corner of the stairwell like I was knotting a homecoming tie, which made him choke with laughter. And he begged me to stop. And so I stopped. What do you make of that kind of love? That kind of desire? And so I held on tighter, enraged. Monica, my girlfriend, couldn't see us. And if she did she would've ran or jumped on him, and scratched him or something. No one else was close to us. And so he said, go ahead, push me all the way down to the landing where the pool is. Nobody will find me there. Go ahead white boy. I'm almost gone. But instead I froze. And gazed into his eyes. Which was a kind of loving. Something broken in it. Something humiliating and sorrowful too. And so I let go. So did he, almost at the same time. And he said to me *I see you* – which to me seemed like love. But it might have been rage, for in that kind of fight between two people the spirit hugs you close. And you feel the heartbeats where love and rage are suddenly one. And nothing but a fight that stops in the gaze of the two eyes can find it in there as a truce. I never saw him again after that. He was lost somewhere. But I heard he was kicked out of the school for carrying a gun. What do you make of that? A boy carrying a gun into a school he didn't belong to? For days afterwards, with Monica, touching her legs as we fooled around, I'd try to *be* his Black hand touching her. The white skin of course, glossed over by Black. And also, how his skin smelled on my two palms afterwards, for we'd held hands together to prevent us from going down the stairs. The smell of his skin. Like leather or something. But sweaty and bright. Oil on leather that keeps up its smell.

The Myth of Fins

In a grassy field, north of the GM-Cadillac Assembly plant a boy
finds an arrow head. A polished relic from the Huron Indians. He
brings it to me. Fingers it in his hand. Aims it straight out. An
arrow head on the Diraga Playground on Dodge Street.
It's winter time. Chromed skies and clouds that puff and stall. And
defeated trees that let the winter winds blow through them. The
street is like a broken puzzle. Car pieces in wreckage.
Large and small metal fragments of the broken arrows we call cars
spread out on the reservation of freeways between
the straights. The city moves a rucksack full of new and broken
arrows. Automobiles on cargo trucks. Smashed ones too.
On flatbeds. We take the Indian arrow head. Twist it in
on ourselves. Aim it at our hearts. Make it impale us so that
we are now both alive with aim and ambition and also killed
at once. We point it high. Stab the gray sky with it. Now it turns
into a magnetic super bird with chrome and wheels. In the myth
of Detroit fins there is a boy who finds an arrow head.
He's small and young but in his mind he designs things.
Feels the head of a Huron Indian rising up in his chest one
afternoon in grade school. He's holding onto the arrow head. It's
in his left hand inside his pocket. Nobody knows it's in there. It's
an odd feeling in him. Like a rising river, bloated with arrow
heads, which the Indian tells him is the myth of fins. And it's the
boy's destiny to flow in it. And be caught in it. And be born in it
and also to be killed in it too, because it is a myth. There is no
escape, because a myth is like a bow that holds
an arrow in place. And it fixes it there until the arrow shoots out,
runs its final course. So the man turns the arrow head around
in his right hand one day in an office in 1953. Makes it a fin
on the rear fender of a car. It's a Dodge D-500.

Also a Plymouth Fury. Later on, he twists and bends it into a torpedo, and he shapes it into the rising shark fin of a 1959 two tone Dodge Custom Royal. Also a black 1958 Desoto Firelight and a 59' Cadillac. I have the myth of fins in me. So do you. All of us who live here in the broken puzzle pieces of the city north and south and east and west of the assembly plant live with the myth of fins inside us. We have the Huron Indian inside our chests too. Sometimes I feel the arrow head in me. I twist it in me. Work it deep into the meat of my heart so I can feel my destiny in there. The act of making something great until it's gone. The driving urge. To roar away. Like cars.

He Helps Me Count
What's Left Behind

I see him in his green taxi cab.
He's idling there on Piquette,
a black man high on weed,
although he's driving people
back to their homes, from
shopping for shoes and hair
products in the stores still left
at Woodward, and Grand Blvd.
I ask him to tell me where
the old Hasting Street sign is,
which was the main line of
old Black Bottom, in Detroit,
where the jazz clubs were,
and where John Lee Hooker lived.
We're just a stone's throw
from the old Fischer Plant #21,
where countless General Motors
car bodies were built by men,
toiling in the summertime heat,
and so I climb into his cab,
and we slowly crawl past
the white, abandoned plant.
He turns, and on an unnamed
street littered with tires, trash,
and old liquor bottles he tells me
this is Hastings Street. Then
we drive down Piquette,
and then down Russell till we
get to Milwaukee, and we
drive through dirty puddles
till we get to a corner, and up,
above us, is the only existing
street sign that's still standing.
It's Hastings Street, at Milwaukee.

And we stand outside of it,
a white and black man, talking
about the clubs of Black Bottom.
Talking about our different lives.
Nothing else is near us. The
sky above is spotted with gray mist.
The street's full of dirty puddles.
He tells me he's selling weed,
cheaply, if I want to buy some.
And that he did time, in the pen,
in 1971 for selling dope. He got
into it after the riots, when he
was just 15 and heard the gun shots.
Then he got out in 1976, came
back to these east side streets
where the clubs, collapsed
in dust under the new highway,
kept on sizzling the blues
under the hiss and fire of car tires,
and so he drives a taxi cab.
I tell him my father played jazz
here, in the clubs, back in the 30's.
He tells me his mother used to
hang out at the clubs, especially
the *Royal Blue Club*, on Russell.
'Man they tore that one down along
time ago,' he says. And that
his auntie was one of those
shake dancers that strutted
and shook their bootie in between
sets. And then he says, 'you know
what I'm talking 'bout – she
was an exotic dancer.' And I
grab his hand, and for no explainable
reason I hug him, and he hugs me
back, as if we were old friends,
long lost brothers in arms
or refugees of this sad city,
counting all that's left behind.

Fist

When I sat on the green bench beside the little black girl
whose name was *Vendetta,* I asked her what her name
meant to her. She was the daughter of a momma from
Alabama, she said, but was being raised by her *gramma,*
who was over there at the carnival stand in Hart Plaza,
buying French fries and hot pretzels. The festival blazed on.
Speed boats cut waves in half. Sail boats mended them.
The buildings of downtown glowed like marble statues.
I was in charge of the world, which someone had told me
was just a set of wheels on a broken axle. My real job
was to look out for the girl whose name was Vendetta.
Her white shoes dangled. She munched cotton candy.
She stroked her arm and brushed all the world off of it.
Some of the world landed on my shoe. Some on her ankle.
Some of the world which will be forever ruined landed
down alongside the green bench for the ants to eat it.
Gramma looked over at us and smiled. Worried but polite.
Some of the world that survives landed on the girl's lap.
She heaved it up and took big bites out of it, said *yum...*
I looked over at it. Wanted some for me. And she gave me
a tug full of the cotton candy. Told me to be careful of it.
That cotton candy fools you 'cause it's soft and it's sticky.
You end up getting hungry for it, and you eat it too fast.
Said her mother named her Vendetta 'cause of her father,
who was a factory rat on the West Side. Didn't know her.
Her brother, whose name was foreboding shadow, pushed
his way into the line and tugged on gramma. Forced his way
against the chain of people and he ran headstrong into it.
We saw him go tumbling down, like pieces of litter bug.
A bag of French fries spilling all over the dirty pavement.
The world that is forever ruined inched a bit closer to us...
The girl shook her head and said some people never learn.
My name which means white fool trying to learn about it,
blended with her name which was Vendetta Against Dad,
and she whispered to me that her name meant *fist holding.*
And she hoisted up the cotton candy. Into the light.

50

Portrait of Miles Davis at the Blue Bird Inn, 1953

The slick, pencil thin heroin addict with the suspicious bird eyes
    darting left and right like they had no home no matter what
    steps across the narrow street out here
on Tireman & Beechwood where the Blue Bird Inn
    bebops at night
and the pick-up musicians in their dark sunglasses gather together,
    arguing that the 2nd and the 4th beats in a 4/4 measure
should be *accentuated* – like the honking, burp of birds
singing in the golden tape reel of autumn trees outside of the club
    where Detroit jazzmen play.
And he stops once to flick with his quick middle finger and thumb
    a cigarette to the side of the curb where a 53' Desoto is parked.
It's a two door, idling curbside, two women outside it
    smoking, and one of them is weeping,
taking turns at it like a riddle while the driver is yanking out
a large string bass from the rear and he's not even bothering
    to listen.
Tucking underneath his overcoat a golden trumpet, Miles saunters
up to the club door, taking the last steps from the old hotel
    he's staying at to kick the junk habit, and the weird itching starts
    up his left arm like a corkscrew of spiders.
The Detroit night is soiled and suffocated with smoke,
    and the lungs of the city, so far from New York, burp and belch
    tar flavored soot. From here, he can see the Fischer Building
    lit up, a bright trophy, and he shudders at the chrome of it,
    the bronze at the top of the building shining like an angel's trumpet
    on fire.
And he thinks he sees demons & angels spiraling like sun spots off
of it which is just the junk he feels seeping out of enraged pores,
    and so he spits, and he curses at it quickly, like a raspy,
    barking black dog. Now, at the door, he enters, looks at the half

moon stage where the drum set echoes at the sound
of feet tap dancing. Two women light cigarettes and laugh.
And he kicks the mud from his boot heel, kicks it twice,
like a man stepping into Detroit, ditching New York behind him.

Diana Ross & The Supremes

It's not only that they had specialized in line dances,
those dark, ebony faced girls just out of high school
caught in the act of their very first chances at love –
but rather that they could sing it like it was ours, too.
All three of them, you know, public housing girls. Girls
we could know, too, in the front seats of our parked cars.
And at the drive in, or outside of the high school doors.
How many of us sang with them as they commanded
stop in the name of love, before you break my heart,
and think it over? And the glossy photographs of them
bundled up like skinny, sexed-up otters in their fur coats
on Grand Boulevard at the studios. And all of the publicity
pictures they endured for us, Florence, Mary, and Diana.
It was no wonder they fell, like a handful of silver glitter
out of the dark band stand that was the frozen night sky.
And it's no wonder, me, standing here writing this epitaph
to them as the winter wind beats away at an old doorway, sprung.
It's no wonder, because Black Bottom was rotting and gone.
And because Diana, with her new night shade flower look,
had become their lead singer, replacing poor Florence.
And because the hits, bursting like so much electric radiation
out of Hitsville, USA, were gems; they were finger rings for us.
I wonder, standing here outside where the old 20 Grand
used to be, whether Diana ever comes back here for a visit?
Maybe she cruises the elm-covered streets in a black limo.
I wonder if the beaten up city deserves one more echo?
I wonder if she glazes the sidewalks with her beauty, humming?
Maybe she carries her jewelry deep in her child's heart.
And her memories of the cold stove, the rats, and the old
life in the projects is forever forgotten by her. And so is
Florence, dead at thirty two of heartbreak. And so are we,
because we once loved her and the girls. They were like
sisters to us. And their voices lifted us, too, on cold winter
days where the snow covered streets, like Warren Avenue
where I write this poem, were empty. And because the poor city,
forgotten about like a hit record still spinning, but ended,

was abandoned, too, by Motown. So that all that's left now
is their sound. It's radiant, stark, and bright. Though you
know it can't be true that Diana forgets us. Not us —
we who lined up to see them sing at the swank supper clubs.
Or maybe it's all of us that can't forget her, and the girls, too,
here in the city where cars rust, but memory never sleeps.

Detroit City Notebook

1980-1986

Sometimes you find yourself in the hours,
and you are in a pile of fitful dreams.
You are a nightshade flower, a large white
bugle, singing a song to the moon.
You are alone in your bed, shaking off
the snake bite of liquor and sadness,
and you are looking out your window,
here, on East Willis, which is a street
in Detroit City made full with the stark,
saturated lives of people on their way up,
or down. And you're looking at a ripe full
moon serenading the hard, glass strewn
street like it's a gypsy, a bright round globe
somehow turned vibrant and aroused.
You think of the moon as a white shield.
You see the moon as one of the spirit fires.
It is full of the thoughts people have
and then let go of, deep into their night,
deep into the event of their lives.
It's full of the projections of lovers who've
shoved their hearts down into stone,
or those who've been lifted up and out
of their streams of darkness into the light.
And you are one of them, about to witness
how it is the future sneaks in and pierces
the present, because destinations can't
tolerate ambiguities, and so we get glimpses
of everything we will get, and carry, and lose.
The thought of this makes you restless,
and you roll over again in your bed,
untuck your body from the sheets. It makes
you remember all the nights before this one.
And you are a kid, walking home from
another drunk night at the bar, a wild one
where you saw a man take the thin arms

of a young woman, a perfumed blond waif
in red lips and a mini skirt, and he shoved
her against a table while the band slaughtered
a song against the blank, windless wall
of the bar. And everything, all of the people
sitting or standing against the chairs,
and all of those smoking outside the bar,
fell or collapsed into the invisible fog
surrounding themselves, their lives,
and nothing was made right or wrong in time.
Everything stayed permanent in smoky haze.
All that was left was a future, like an ark,
welcoming whatever gets made into its hand.
And you saw the man kiss her hard, right
there where her mouth opened, then shut,
and they quarreled for their reasons.
And darkness or light filled their mouths.
Every fight is a fight between presence
and absence. What wins, is the notebook,
the fixed, jagged line of a life telling events
backwards, from where things started up.
Now you are out here, outside 27 East Willis,
and you are studying the way the street lights
mix with the strangled throat of the night.
You hear lovers quarreling, and a woman
is playing her piano above you like one of the angels,
one of the lost, bewildered winged ones
forgotten by God, and now she's playing the keys
just to be *found* again, from under the shadows.
You feel the cars as you walk toward Woodward.
A junkie, which is a ghost trying to negotiate
the doorway between permanence and absence,
collapses against a fence, shoots up, nods out.
A woman in a window reads a book,
and you too, feel your body is a book,
a text of movable images all crowding against
the bindings, as if clamoring for their time
and light. Your fingers feel your ribs, feel
all it is that is moving in there, all the selves

caught in there, between the now and the whenever.
The spirit moves blankly, between the fixed,
broken down cars of East Willis.
You leave your self to see it, and the moon,
and all of the men and women you will see
losing their hearts and souls to the notebook,
to the hard scrabble negotiation, of life.

Marvin Gaye & the Wrecking Ball

Driving past the long vacated
service Envelope Manufacturing Company, Inc,
   at the I-94 and I-75 junction,
right where the two highways
   intersect in the old factory district of Detroit,
and where you can see ruin
East and west, and salvage yards
   piled with heaps of scrap metal and smoky fires
seeming to burn for no apparent reason,
   I see the billboard to Marvin Gaye.
How strange to see him here, overlooking
   the freeway and Dubois street,
where the grassy fields and abandoned houses
   light up with the sudden flaring
of wild pheasants and drunks, waking up.
The billboard's got his large, intense face there.
Those eyes, looking out over the freeway,
   like they're pools of suspicion and sexual hunger.
It's his early 70's face, bearded, masculine,
   with a hint of feminine sexual vulnerability,
like he's looking to you for something,
   for some affection, or for some freebie.
So much ruined promise in Marvin....
The preacher father who beat him senseless
   as a boy to get him right with God.
The torment he felt, between spirit and sex,
   the cocaine addiction, the women.
So much ruin in Marvin, and in Detroit,
   how the gun shot ruins them both.
How they're both under the wrecking ball...
   I can picture Marvin, arms spread across his bed,
   that big sad face buried there in his grief,
thinking of the night Tammie collapsed in his arms
   during a set in Virginia,
how it was death started after him, through her.
Well, to be fair, death had been after him

all his life. Even the song cycles hint at it.
But for death to grab at Tammi,
   right there, during the ecstasy of music
must have proved the inevitable to Marvin.
The songs that followed hint at the ruin,
   what's going on…
Yesterday, I stood outside the old Motown building
   on Woodward, at I-75. The old offices.
The outside of the building blue,
you'd always know it when you went by it.
There, outside the building, was a young Marvin,
   a look alike in a hoodie,
a dope fiend, watching the shadows.
He and I watched a crane swinging its arm,
and a wrecking ball blasting that building
   to history.
History is the song cycle that Detroit humiliates.
Nothing here is preserved. It's all destroyed.
It's all thrown away for parking spaces,
   as if nothing beautiful had been wrung out of voices
   in a musical studio, and no one beautiful
lived here long enough to penetrate the absence,
   and so the only noise left is the demolition
   of it, like an excessive beating on an empty drum.
It's the preacher and the wrecking ball,
   swinging madly at the old, gloried building
with the afternoon sunlight glinting off of it,
   the dust, reaching a high ugly arm
   up into the failed, afternoon city light.
And Marvin, high on coke, stumbling into the dust,
   away.

Two Men Watching Martha Reeves
& the Vandellas Exit the 20 Grand

We stood at the back door of the 20 Grand
on Warren and Grand Boulevard while the sky
pelted us with dirty rain squalls through the empty trees
and nobody who was drunk ruined anything else,
and the police cars muscled away to the east side.
When we saw them leave by the back door
in their white satin gowns and their lips silvered,
you nudged me to look through my broken glasses
because all that rises by gold and silver and spins
on the turntable – all this music, this laughter,
this history, all this glorious fortune – will stop
in a fade-out as the tip of the needle, bouncing
on word and melody, blunts out, and nothing else
except the skipping of it lasts. We are a religion
of dance music and green reefer. And when you
light it up and pass it to me, I choke on it and I laugh
until my ribs are a blind pig. And the bird in my
chest, who wears a carnival clown's face and is
the reason why I am drunk and bewildered and full
of antebellum wordplay and greased slapstick,
flies high above my head, and it flaps its oil soot wings
until it clears the chimney tops choked in grit,
and something like my whole history falls into dark pieces.
Sometimes you light a bible on fire to get a good buck.
Sometimes it costs us our own teeth to get a laugh.
And the girls, here on the Boulevard and Warren,
climb like three queens into an idling limousine
as the stars above us all race into drenched smoke.
And the rich people whose lives are invisible
to us, and who are of politics and Wall Street, and
whose shoes are made of Italian leather for waltzing,
and whose women are delighted and laughing
as they scoop arms with their men and leave us
to our flop-houses-of-gin and rain-squalid blues,
leave by droves to their secret little kitchens again.

You won't let me forget this night and the way
we fell into our future of nothingness and jokes.
Don't forget the way we laughed away our sadness
to jokes and Jesus and the way we kissed the girl,
each one of us as she stroked her thigh for us.
All of that, and those nights we stumbled out
to hear Martha and the girls sing and dance for us.
And smoke the evenings of this city into closed
boxes and love letters. And all the other broken,
beauty things.

At the Rinaldo Arms Manor, an Obituary

Everything that is related to beauty should be unaffected by the passage of time

Simone Weil

i

In 1985, at the Rinaldo Arms Manor,
a man, a plumber, *a drunk*, twisted up, into
himself, and he died alone in his bed.
It was the summer time, hot, humid,
and his big body, being just a servant
to God, and to the Devil of sinfulness
and pridefulness, gave over to the greedy,
brutal hand of gravity as it fisted up...
It took him down as quickly and quietly
as a terrible hand snatches daylight.
My brother and I didn't know that he'd died
until an Asian woman told us, by playing her piano.
When you die, your body, which is
a landmass, just a buildup of defense
and hunger, settles down like mud...
And the fire, which is a witch, or
a lady from your past, sets you ablaze...
You're consumed in the soul's fire.
We didn't know that, because we
were young, and we didn't know
that death stalks you in *five* forms,
and then there is one extra, a *sixth*,—
and that one is from *love*,
which always fools the survivors,
because death by love's like an *elopement*,
you die by eloping. A man dying alone
of liquor isn't eloping, he's dreaming
of rabid dogs.

The six ways of dying fool everybody.
And so the first is *bitterness*, the way that
a worm invades an apple, and the second
is by *murder*, which is when a certain
shadow falls like a blade across a floor,
and nothing can change it; it's the way
that life arranges forms to change shape,
into superstition and evil; into degradation.
And because we were young and we didn't
believe that everything was just a formula
of energy being changed into new matter,
my brother and I never gave it any thought.
And the third way of dying is by *infidelity*,
which is the way one form contaminates another,
like two chemicals in unholy matrimony,
and when they mix, there is saturation,
which completes the evanescence of the one.
And the fourth way of dying is through
random chaos, which is life's way of shuffling
the cards. And the fifth form of dying
is by *apathy*, which is the method life uses
to apply the laws of justice to that of someone
full of dread; you know, of what he *is*,
of what he's *becoming*; by the dent of his own
debauched will…So the house flies,
sweltering over the counter top and the rancid
butter dish, swelled above the dead plumber
like he was a big, wooden Ouija board…
We didn't know anything, because we were
just trying to figure out our small lives.

There was a woman, an Asian woman
who knew that the plumber died. And –
in her turn – because she'd been emotionally
involved with Beethoven's *Moonlight Sonata*,
which is one way that moonlight invades
a woman, fills her heart with lust and
with ineligibility, and with fidelity
and rage and Eros, and with Beethoven's
particular obsession with impotence,
she pounded on her piano that evening,
because it was the only thing she could do.
And that is because she was impassioned.
She was a lover snapping rays of light
in between her quick-moving fingers.
She was a musician, or a night poet.
If she had a man, we didn't know it.
Her lips were red, they were bleeding
with beauty. There's no other way to say it.
Nobody in the hallway knew her,
except that she dragged her groceries
up the lonesome stairs in a metal cart.
And she unlocked the sad door to her
place like a white ghost with red lips…
And that is what red lipstick is, it is
the blood of a woman and who will
salve it – because it's a wound and a
long drink of white light turned red,
and nothing but harmony can save her,
can bring her back to a contented heart.
So she was pounding her piano keys
with the *Moonlight Sonata*, in Detroit,
on the evening that we found the plumber,
dead of combustion in his room.
The hallway was flushed with death,
all of the five forms of dying plus the sixth…
We listened hard, astonished at her power.
And we couldn't leave the city, either,

because we were poor, and its inhabitants,
and we were prisoners of the sixth form
of dying – which is *love*. So we cupped
our ears to the doorway, trying to hear
what it was she was playing. The rising
and falling of keys, the milky glow
of moonlight in the hall, everything,
all of it, surrounding the dead plumber.
We listened to the lamentation she
was playing. She was trying to elope
like Beethoven did, with God.

Elegy for the Residents
of the Niagara Apartments

I

Because there are stories too disturbing to retell
I have to first talk about the field of yellow flowers

growing like orphans in the wild, tangles of grass
outside of the Niagara Apartments on 3rd Avenue.

And I have to tell about Fortune Records at 3942
3rd Avenue, just north of Seldon, and the day I went

in there, panting on a run downtown, and I saw the rows
of record bins full to the edges with rare, hard to get vinyl.

There was Nolan Strong and the Fabulous Diablos
sitting up on the wall, I think it was 'Mind over Matter,'

and there was 'Adios, My Desert Love,' too,
and Andre Williams howling out 'Bacon Fat,'

and of course there was John Lee Hooker,
his head tucked down into the sweaty darkness

of a club scene in Paradise Valley, who knows what year,
but it must have been in the years he lived on Orleans.

Because I can't reveal your secret decrepitude
Lawrence, Don and Marilyn, Norman, Mary, Rosie,

all of you huddling around an egg white electric burner
with burnt coffee on it, in winter, I'll recall the stale liquor

on your breath, and the stench of cigarettes
and the urine in the hallway where one light bulb

blown out, looked like an extinguished planet,
and none of you noticed what God himself missed,

which was the thin streak of plaster breaking open
to reveal another world, darker and more sinister,

and the roach crawling like a secret blemish into it,
which must have revealed that even roaches here, go to Hell.

    II

All of you in the hard years climbed into that crack on the wall.
And that's because, when I went running past you,

and I saw you stuck like statues in the wild grasses,
the wind billowing through your weary, tired clothes,

the blue sky above, fluffed alive with clouds, I knew
that you were offerings, nothing more, to the larger

code of decay here, where just down street, at Peterboro,
a dog was bent over, brown as leather, and chewing

on something red, and I think I saw you there, Mary,
your wrist always broken and in a white cast, feeding

the pigeons too, because they were your only children,
and because there were no more prayers left to say.

And because poverty is the way that God transmits the code
of loss and ruin, throughout the kingdoms, and into the people.

III

When they tore the Niagara Apartments down, long after
I'd left there, I'm sure all of you were almost dead and gone.

Poverty is the explanation of what happens to a soul without
mercy or love, which I think all of us here can all agree with,

and when the demolition crews and their aggressive shovels
dug out dirty dishes and silver pans, I'm sure they found

Norm's filthy converse sneakers and his TV, and I'm sure Mary's
silver walker and Rosie's key set were ground into weeds

and into drip board pilings and bricks, and I'm sure the last
drunken quarrel between Don & Marilyn was echoing

through the steel girders and the window moldings as they
were ripped down, and they fell into dirt and concrete,

and into the walls with wiring scoring out of them like hair. And
I'm sure the vast story of your lives, although lonely and secretive,

could be heard as one alive song, and it was the song of the yellow
flowers blowing wild and free in the spring grasses on 3rd Avenue

between Charlotte and Peterboro, where the city workers
in their yellow construction hats were bending over in debris,

their gloved hands ruffling through it all, and they were collecting
invisible bits of each and every one of your souls.

John Lee Hooker's Boogie Chillun

I

Beneath the Dequindre Cut, full of greased weeds & graffiti,
you can see the exact spot where roaming dogs shit,

and lovers, because they're expressions of musical notes & lust,
kiss like lovers kiss, one after another in the front seat

of an old Pontiac, here in the pinguid filth of the Eastern Market
where the slaughter houses and the lamb skin factories

stinking of dead animal carcasses and salt, combine on Orleans
and Monroe Street, so that John Lee can arrive, with a bruised guitar

in a box, the Devil skulking behind him, sometime in 43.'
And he can squat in a shack, gone now, long gone in the years

that act like razor blades cutting every shack to bits.
Except for Sam, the guy I talk to, who tells me in busted apart

English because he's from the Deep South and he's 73 years old
and his back teeth – the ones that can grab hard on tobacco

and on hard-to-say-words – are old chunks of dead weight, well,
he can tell me that he still lives in a dusty wooden shack,

just off of St. Aubin, where there's a view of the slaughter house
and John Lee's place, even though it's long gone now.

And even though the woman he slept with, in the old 47' Pontiac,
is nothing now except the particulate of dandelions & black ink.

II

Where it is written that the boogie chillun swing on Hastings Street
John Lee, dark as coal burning in an oven, can sing it,

and you can feel it as heat rising up a fence line, weeds crowding it,
and you can see it as flame bursting out of a rigid chimney stack.

And all the young, festooned girls, portable young things ready
to submit to the anything that guides them like rolling black stars

skipping across the sidewalks of Russell Street & Beaubien,
and then on to Henry's Swing Club, on Orleans, you can see them

now as the gnarled trees & weeds under the Dequindre Cut.
And some graffiti artist down there, a quick moving pulsar of light,

is spray painting the future, because it was always hungry to get here,
and you can go down there, amidst the blown tires & the mattresses

and the old car chassis, and find the boogie chillun, their throats parched
and thirsty from the hot weight of the night, their roots sucking oil.

III

Ladies & Gentleman of the cornucopias of littered trash, of forgotten
auto hulks never mentioned, of slaughtered animals glazed in blood,

of the wantonness of soiled floors where knife blades divide ribs,
I want to tell you of the boogie chillun, John Lee's kin, yours & mine,

because they are the ones born in music and the ones lost in light,
and they are the ones whose voices go on singing in the low wind

that's wandering like a melody under Alfred Street Bridge, where Sam's
walking this morning, his mouth full of chewing tobacco and blues,

and I am walking there with him, one of the free ones never a part
of the 1943 riots that slaughtered this town like a lamb's neck.

And we're getting high on the light that's slanted like a guitar string
through the wreckage of a viaduct, he & I, and we're not alone.

We're never never alone, he shouts out at no one, we're never alone,
our roots and toots live inside the ashes and underneath the weeds,

and he throws his arms up in arrivals & in cataclysmic gestures, and
in soiled lathered sweat; we're never alone, he shouts out to no one,
never alone.

Song of Detroit

I saw Antoine Laumet de Lamoth Cadillac sucking on sweet grass &
    oil at Hart Plaza.
I saw swarms of mosquitoes and mississauga snakes eating Belle Isle.
I saw the attack of the Ottawa Indians & the Miami & their bones
    in a Buick.
I saw the British soldiers defeat the French & the Indians & open a pub,
    and then I saw Chief Pontiac, face red as dirt, stabbed to death,
    drunk.
I saw Commander John Francis Hamtramck get drunk at Wheeler's Bar
    on Joseph Campau in the town they later named after him.
    Half the bones from his face missing and the liquor draining
    down an empty neck.
I saw Father Gabriel Richard genuflecting in a pool of blood at St. Anne's
    Church.
I saw Augustus B. Woodward sipping fresh cocktails with Berry Gordy Jr.
I saw Hazen S. Pingree swatting pigeons away and rioting drunks throwing
    flames at Black motorists in the 1943 riots. White lover girls mixing
    with Black musicians at the Algiers Motel, 1967.
I saw the Savoyard River, thick with walleye, turn into a sewer ditch.
I saw Lewis Cass selling off parcels of land & a heroin addict buying junk
    on the street.
I saw Henry Ford offer $5 a day to Southern Blacks and the Apple
    of Discord go rolling like a yo yo across a wooden plank floor at
    Ford Motor.
I saw Packard, Dodge, Desoto, Fischer Plant #21 turn into metal & oil
    zones, and hundreds of sweaty workers eating greased ball bearings
    for lunch, their shoulders slumped, their heads hung low, ashamed.
    Joe Louis's big fist.
I saw a night curfew called in Detroit and troops storm Black rioters, 1943
    & 1967.
I saw Black Bottom oil and coal smoke. I saw black blood mixed with
    Indian.
I saw white women sewing up the hems of stitched corpses & orphan
    annie slave girls.

I saw black men and white women seeking comfort in each other's arms.
I saw the eyeless dolls on Tyree's Heidelberg Street like unconsciousness
    nightmares glued to the houses.
    The street full of grocery carts, mannequins, polka dots.
I saw homeless men in Capitol Park stretch into griffons & land on the
    Book Cadillac & also on the razed Madison-Lennox, the
    Penobscot, like dark angels.
I saw Gratiot, Marlboro, Oakland Avenue, Seward, Superior, Jefferson
    Avenue turn into burning bricks with howling mouths & epitaphs
    & tombs, and dark hearses carrying the bones of union strikers to
    Mayor Jeffries.
I saw the 67' Riots turn into a humiliated battle between the blacks and the
    cops. The fires up Clairmont and 12th like 4th of July fireworks,
    whites running away.
I saw the Devil's Night fires consume whole streets as I drove down a
    freeway.
I saw the Eastern Market swarming with live fish, slaughtered steer,
    bloodied lambs, Russell Street paint-balled with vegetables, fruits,
    peanut shells, blood. And Sam's Cut Rate, Kerns, Cunninghams &
    Woolworths get the wrecking ball. Grand Circus Park lose all of its
    movie theaters, burlesque houses, nobility.
I saw Yusef Lateef blowing a saxophone amidst the street fires on Russell
& Mt. Elliott. Paul Chambers, Elvin & Thad Jones going with
Miles & leaving the city. All the clubs – the 606, The Cozy Corner,
    Club Plantation, Klien's Show bar, shut.
And all the rest of Paradise Valley up Hastings & John R get dug out
    for a highway.
I saw Nolan Strong & the Fabulous Diablos on the wall at Fortune
    Records. Jackie Wilson screaming & jig-sawing across a stage as
    dark crows surrounded his head.
I saw Diana Ross & the Supremes, The Marvelettes, The Temptations, &
    Marvin Gaye recording at Hitsville, the air on fire, thousands of
    people begging, clapping, Boston Blvd and Chicago Blvd glittery
at Christmas time. Barry Gordy & Smokey moving to LA, all the
rest of us, left here, damaged, to stay, smoldering.

I saw the infatuation of Madonna, Bob Seger & Iggy blowing glass, chests
    pumped,
I saw the White Stripes, the Contours, Stevie Wonder & the MC5
hit it big.
    Eminem & Kid Rock genuflecting at the Gold Dollar & to
    8 Mile.
I saw strip malls decimate the downtown sector, white businessmen
    blowing it up.
Greektown turn into a loud gambling mecca full of thumping SUVs.
    The Southwest Side fill up with Latino eateries & gangs on
    Junction & Clark Streets & the great Michigan Central Train
    Depot become an art museum of graffiti & animal bones.
    The Lee Plaza Hotel hoisting up a piano in a purple fist of
    twisted smoke.
I saw Hudsons explode, a billion old bridal registries bursting into
confetti, divorces —
The 7 sisters fall down like the smokestacks of hell into the white wash
of the Detroit river.
Delray & all the down river side streets turn into a stinking waterway of
    ruin along the Rouge.
    The effigies of the Tigers, Pistons, Lions, Red Wings bronzed &
    burned.
The house I was born in blown up in a billowing fire ball of smoke.
    My high school close.
I saw all the highways in & out of here painted Devil's Night red,
    rainbowed in blood.

Grand River Avenue, Detroit Riots, 1967

Sometimes in a young mind there are rabbits sniffing pine cones
and wet grass in the morning. The world is an aural landscape
of meditative beauty. In my young mind I'm driving with my father.
I'm not sure where in the hell we're going. It is July, 1967,
and there is smoke billowing out of roof tops. Army vehicles,
which look like big violent bugs, churn forward down the streets.
I'm told to duck down in the station wagon. I'm told there could be
sniper fire. My young head could be blown apart like milkweed.
So I grip the back of the seat with my strong arms like I'm hugging
the side of a wall for protection. My stomach, which is full of acid
and stones, tightens. My father looks ahead as if sniffing down
a long corridor to a doorway, something golden and light.
I'm guessing he's looking straight into Heaven, for I am Catholic,
and I can't guess ahead to anything else. Nothing but white light.
And there are angels, big weeping winged things caressing
the burning cars exploded down along the side streets. Some angels
genuflect. Some blow saxophones or trumpets and they throw
them down on the street loudly. And it sounds like wailing or crying,
as if all of Heaven's gate had fallen like glass over us. Then I peek up,
see the black men running away. Some of them run into store
fronts with no glass remaining. And their faces are terrified ripped pieces
of rubber. And the police cars race forward after them. Fire trucks
roar down the road and blow hoses full of water all over them.
Someone calls them devils but it sure isn't my father, for his heart
is as wobbly as a bowl of milk and he respects them. And the angels,
which are large insects with beating wings and wailing faces that resemble
sun flowers bursting apart, race and swoop down on us. And one of them
cradles the window of the car like a blanket, a large bursting mouth
of howling. And he yells at me you will be named John one day
and you will tell of the apocalypse here. And every story you tell will
be true. And bewildering. For you fear all this and it breaks your heart.

Sculpture

– 12th Street & Clairmont

The old men sit on the benches
here in the simple little park
on 12th and Clairmont where
the riots exploded in 1967.
You must wonder why I think
so much of these riots a man
says to me. No, I'm saying it
to you. I have a pen inside my
finger. It keeps writing words
so the silenced ones can speak.
The riots never ended, he says.
And I hear the echo inside me.
The Devils Night fires in the 1980's
were the children of Hermes,
says the dark philosopher king.
They say a place burning itself alive
is a place whose funeral is king.
All the love lust goes into dying.
Maybe something else gets born in it.
Maybe the woman in it is a plague.
A vortex of mayhem and riot.
Something of her womb on fire.
Something of her fingers eat light.
The woman at the wig shop
with gold teeth says her mother
carried a child through the blaze.
The riots never did end for her,
she says to me, lighting up a smoke.
Points to herself and says, *me.*
All the voices cling to the trees.
Every hand carries a switch blade.
Every heart an humiliation in it.
Every mind a yellowed story page.
Every soul a torched horoscope.
Every child hungry expectant eyes.
The music of a blaze never leaves

says the fire truck roaring by me.
The fate of a place is where it fades
says the car company going dark.
All the buildings make profits
for the King and his mistress to
chew on, lovers of magic and speed.
They leave the banquet hall empty.
They spit on the place as they leave it.
You can never ignore the history
of a place says the tiny sculpture
standing alone in the park. Never
because it lives on what you feed it.

Elegy for Whatever isn't Right

One after the other the boys grew tired of shooting hoops.
And so they'd punch one another and sip on the liquor
one of them stole from his grandfather, and they'd climb
on a dirty bicycle, a two wheel stingray, silver, with a flag
and they'd circle around the glass, crackled like fallen stars
on the street. Then one of them would go fetch a pistol,
just a simple Glock 9mm and he'd challenge the others to take bets
on what he could shoot at, for instance a bird on a wire,
or a couch, rotting on the curb side, or a wrecked car.
Sometimes he'd shoot at a house, just for kicks, and they'd
take bets on how many windows they could shoot out.
Sometimes they'd ambush a stray dog and shoot him dead.

~

In the middle of the summer they'd get bored and restless
so they'd pile in a car and drive to the festivals held on the river.
You'd always find crowds there, white and black, and it was
good business for pick pocketing or hassling suburban kids
who didn't know their asses from a sewer hole and so they'd
brandish the pistol and corner some group of boys wearing
baseball caps and kakis and they'd push them around a bit,
shove them up against one of the bathroom walls or something,
just enough to scare them, and they'd rob the boys blind
and walk off laughing. They'd never run. Just walk off laughing.

~

Sometimes the words auto, and auto parts, and machinery,
or assembly line at $5 per day, the brand new Model T,
or men in overalls full of pine oil and dirt with axes
hacking away at the trees until they were falling giants
would appear on the pages of history books in school.
And the names Dodge, Buick, Durant, Ford, Chevrolet
would all gather together as the forefathers of the city.
The boys never understood any of this because it seemed
like ancient history, and so they'd yawn through it,
and chew on candy bars in class and smoke bud after.

During one of the festivals a girl, just 14, had a child,
quickly during the part of the festival where the jazz
was loudest and rambunctious, which was good, very good,
because then the girl, because she was the youngest
daughter of commotion, would always associate
the birth of her child with music, tom toms beating wildly
and trumpets spanking the hot dog smells and the smoke
over the river and past the hovering white people
drinking on their power boats, and cheating on each other.

~

Then, as the trajectory of smoke wafted south east, toward
the east side where gunshots were fired across side streets
as one gang fought for the turf of another gang, for coke
and for the wreckage of an old house banged empty,
engines, wheels, alignment shops, radiator shops, gear
joints, saloons, Christian bible stores, afro-centric book
stores, food marts, burger joints, auto glass shops, boat
stores, marinas, everything, all of it, because they were smoke
now and the ruined pieces of a city, all formed the puzzle
pieces of a road map, a collection of stories being sold off.
It was just pocket change for whomever won it, took it
for a part of the larger battle ground that was the war,
and so the boys, all of them, figured one day they'd be
part of it like their older cousins, their uncles, all their kin.

~

Now and then, the boys would see all this and rap to it,
or forget about it since there was nothing in their songs
that could solve any of it, and so they'd push and shove
each other, and drive to the malls and buy hoodies, sports
clothing, bling. Then, in September, one of the boys,
because he was the child's father, and the boyfriend to
the girl who'd had the baby in the summer time, was
stabbed in the neck by another boy, a kid who'd carried a
pocket knife all summer and practiced slashing the leaves
off of a bush like he was cutting the ears off a stray cat,
and from that point on it was war, one way or another.
And the war was about pride, or something like it.

79

~

Because this story is about how a kingdom is purchased
by testing and challenge and violence, I have to tell the rest
of it, because of the girl. So she'd fall asleep on an old cot
while the baby child wailed and her grandmother, a Baptist,
would rock the child in her old arms and pray out loud
and tell the girl she was a two bit street whore and a mistake,
and the single reason for badness. And the boy who had
practiced cutting the leaves off of shrubs all summer, because
he was another mistake, would hide in the bushes, waiting
for the time he'd be killed by the group of boys with a gun.
The reason he would wait was because he was the girl's brother.

~

After Ford opened the first factory, at Mack Avenue & Bellevue,
others followed, and Detroit became world class in production.
There were malleable iron manufacturers, gear shops, markets,
transmission shops, iron works, cigar stores and dime stores.
It was here, on an autumn day, that the boys, about eight
of them, cornered the boy with the knife and gunned him down.
Most of it was based in a vendetta, but some of it was accident.

Just the wages of war between boys with nothing better to do.
Nothing greater to believe in, and so the girl, because it's
her story, would get sent back to Alabama where her kin
were from, and she'd work all the next summer after that,
while rocking the child in her arms and calling him *bazo zola*,
which is African for someone whose body is love & fire,
like the explosion of fireworks over the river at the festival.
And she'd promise to do right by him, because he was hers
and her brother's, she figured, and that boy who did the
shooting too, who was the father, the child was his, too –
although he was in jail now, or dead, she didn't know.
And so she'd carry the child in a papoose, out through the
cotton to a big old tree with a swing on it, and they'd swing
and she'd sing to the child until her mouth was dry with her
own saliva and salt. And when the sun would set she'd hear
the tom toms, beating, and she'd see the first stars, one
after another rising, like piles of glass on the dark city street.

80

And she'd promise the boy to do right by him because
she was the daughter of commotion, she was a trumpet,
her young body felt like it had the holy ghost burning inside it —
something in her rib cage was exploding into fierce light.
It was just the story of survival she and her son would live.
And because her badness, whatever it was, wasn't right.

Sports

I remember the fight with that boy who broke my nose.
How the blood on my face and my arm bubbled up
and out of me like a strange puddle of red roses.
How good I felt inside myself because of my wounds
and my bravery. How I'd take it with me into sports.
How I'd learn to run into any kind of wind for my city.
Love and strife are the bed mates inside all victories.
Perhaps all contact wounds on my skin are in fact
the blood and rose bushes of my actual soul nudging up
from the depth of my rib cage as an act of self-revelation.
How long it must take for the soul to admit to itself
that it's stuck now in the corporeal! And so I watched
all those days ago when Jim Northrup hit the grand slam
homer in the 1968 World Series game between Detroit
and St Louis. How that grand slammer was a celebration
for my poor city whose skin had been ruptured open
by the riots. Everyone who lived here knew it! Felt it!
How the victory tasted sort of like blood lust and blue sky.
I think for a week the soul of the city rose up in confetti.
How I raced down Westbrook Street in a kind of jubilation,
raising my young fists. And I felt that pride inside myself
because I knew then that nothing good ever comes
to anyone without its hard price. How young I was
to know something as valuable as this! The Red Wings
and the Pistons too. How their trophies shine like silver rings
on a city's bruised fingers. How they glisten like gold teeth
inside the beat up mouth of a wounded place trying to smile.
And how I remember elbowing that boy on the track
later on in the two mile race. And I felt my blood burst
out of my calf muscle when he spiked me with his cleats.
How I won the race anyway. And I hugged him
later on because it was worth it to make a new friend.
And because, I knew I was racing for my city. My soul.

The City is a Woman

Said the man on Forest Avenue.
He was holding his brown bag
of fortune & his eyes were salt.
Do you know she loves the body
of a man even though he's beat
her? All this as the gulls rose up
over the black chimney towers
and the trucks stomped & rolled
into the Eastern Market district.
To love a woman, I think, is to
try out for size what it is to be
a swollen watermelon. The heart
is full of redness and dark seeds.
There are stories & dark truths.
Murder and mayhem and a laughter
that is really a strange card game.
We take our chances when we
love someone until the end of it.
The heart of a city, this one, is full
of coughing & dead radiators,
and men whose time is a lottery.
The women in it grow dark & mute
and hum songs to hanging laundry
that is never fully cleaned off.
The children in it are leaving it.
We must remember that the city
is a woman, he said.

Beautiful Rust

Standing underneath the Ambassador Bridge, shrouded in fog, I find
a metal chip, a rusted fragment. I hold it in my fingers, lift it up
like it is a found piece of my body. This is at Composite Forging, a factory
on Fort Street and 14th, where a man in a beard works a hi-low, moves it
across mud. Lifts metal tubes, drives them into a pine green building
where men, amorphous shapes, step in, pull them off, load them, leave.
I watch him until I am a rusted figure. Someone drowned in fog and rain.
Someone entirely lost inside a myth of fins and rusted metal.
And in a city drenched in something complete and incomplete at once.
In my body there is a blood rust river. It is my bloodline. All my relations
live here, metal pieces of rust. Beautiful rust. I pick up the metal chip.
Slice it across my middle finger till I split apart. Watch the blood bursting
out of me, rusted, acidic. Something in me is so dead I can't even find me.
Something so rusted I am like a tin man. Heartless. Stuck and stranded
in a muddy factory parking lot. So out of breath I am stiff and frozen,
in a grave. Without anything close to me I can even love. Be loved by.
The cars roar by me, choking the city's eyes. Exhausting its haggard lungs.
I watch the blood spill down across my open palm until I let it bleed
into the soggy soil beneath my boot heel. Now I watch the mud sip it,
my blood rust. All this beautiful rust cut open, spread across my palm –
as if the heart in me, still and frozen, rusted, could pulse awake again,
my arteries lit up. Alive. In the beautiful rust there are a thousand faces
I know. They come. Go. Some are on my fingertips. Some nothing
anymore. Just metallic dust. Some, the rules we live by until something
else, another rule, takes us over. Now I watch me bleed down into the earth
again. Watch my blood rust sink down into wet mud where it can touch
the darker soil, and the lighter soil, curled up inside it, and sitting brightly
in the wet filth. Something fans awake inside me. Something else goes slack,
slithers back down in. Finds its trusting path into the silent caverns
where all my blood rust drains. Finds itself awake again. Vital. Where all
the cities breathe.

Falling in Love, 1986

– for Anita, of course

i

It is a burden, this living alone.
At night, feet up on your dirty balcony,
drinking your 40 ounce beer,
you think about the usual topics,
like women and men and sadness,
or, for instance, like whether the stars
hanging over Detroit like copper gears,
or like the souls of drive shafts
or pistons, will ever quiver and rumble
inside your chest for someone you love.
For somebody special, and equal to you.
And you dwell on your own sadness,
and how it's a small glowing
fungus blotch on your heart or lung.
You actually think hard about this.
And though it feels soft and weak,
like used up tissue after a break-up,
it's really mostly made of toughness,
like wadded up tear balls or spit;
and it's full of the self-assurance
that you're unhappy, and so it captures
you, and it fools you with its beauty
because it shines, too, whenever
you drink too much and look hard at it,
deep down inside of yourself. You know,
after everything else has turned quiet;
after all the women have gone home,
and you're a little bit too drunk
to listen, or to figure out what you're
really trying to say to yourself,
and so you falter a bit, and try to sleep.

The cars, moving in packs uptown,
shine on like they're spheres of jewelry,
or like bursting, quick prisms of light.
Sometimes you see them leaping
on the movie screens of your eye lids
long after they're gone, and you're in bed.
And your eye lids blink off like television.
The woman you love is driving
to meet you. She's on the Lodge Freeway,
journeying from the far West Side, to here.
You think for hours about kissing her.
In her mouth there's a special name
she has for you. It's only for you
and you can't really believe it, because
falling in love is like a new name.
When you stretch out in your bed,
arms spread behind your neck,
you think that the name in her mouth
will be the final name on the other side
of sadness, where there can be no end
or beginning to anything new,
because it's only a name in the *now*.
And falling in love can only happen
over and over again in the now.
When you think of her,
driving down the highway to meet you,
you absently touch your ear lobes.
They're like two ringing church bells.
It's because she has a name for you,
and it's chiming like a wedding in there.
And you drag your hand through your
hair just to hear something different.
Then you run your finger across your lips,
just to touch where you will kiss her.
Sometimes, alone on your balcony,
drinking your beer and thinking
of her, you get a brand new taste

in your mouth and it tastes like gold.
Her mouth is a red two lane highway.
A two lane you can drive away on.
In your mouth, where the broken
down images of the city are chewed
up in hunger or in sadness or in anger,
all the junkies and the beat up girls
you taste in there, are gone.

Green
– for Margo

The man whose fingers are made of dark mud
and clay kneels down again, digs his fingers into the earth
like the set of his fingers are knobby worms nosing
away from the dawn's light into the moist garden soil,
as if wiggling down to home. Above him, a red cardinal
strokes the low gray sky with a sudden color, lands
up in the branches of a maple tree, begins its singing.
Trucks on Harper and Gratiot thunder on already,
and the old woman who waters her pots of geraniums
on the front porch waves at him, coffee in hand.
One by one the little boys and girls who help him garden
line up above him, eager little sprites, skinny as celery,
knees ready to fall down into the soil, to dig and weed.
The man pulls up a radish, pink, moist, drops it into
the pail. Moves down a row, cultivates the soil again,
pats and caresses the earth woman beneath his hands
like he and the earth are in something like a partnership,
like they are dear lovers or something like old friends.
And he pours the smooth water into her mud again,
as if giving her a cold long drink, like a Mother's Day
gift. Dawn splits open above the downtown buildings,
carrying a light across the garden and the fruit trees.
His knees nudge the earth, as if he is climbing back
into something primal in himself, some old way of living.
A dog barks, a cat wiggles through the fence line,
runs at something underneath a wood pile, stops, sniffs.
Wind carries a sweet breeze he recalls feeling as a boy.
He used to work at Chrysler. Made parts for cars.
Nothing in his memory of that except that men make parts
for other men to sell, and now he is loving something
else, a mud and green world where his hands, just worms,
cultivate the soil, make edibles, dig and pat the body
of a woman, Detroit, and grow food for her children –
whose eyes are hungry, and gaze at him like dark beans.

Our Common Souls

Outside, on this spring day under the blue sky's
   ordinary brilliance,
and invited by an exploring wind nudging lost papers
   forward pell-mell on a street called St. Aubin,
which was named after the saint
   that ransomed slaves, and fed the sick and the indigent,
I come across a cook-out,
a barbecue at the True Vine Temple of Christ Church —
here in the battleground we call Detroit City,
   just a few miles north of downtown, and it's nothing
larger than a brick storefront,
this church of saved souls, Gospel music
   ecstatically blaring out of stereo speakers,
and friendly, contented people, eyes bright, urging me in.
     ~

I stop, and I'm fed and welcomed and tended to
   by black folks as sunny as this May light
spreading a celebration over the street
   and over a house, blackened by arson, and gutted
   down to floor planks and sooty half-walls.
Across the street boys push and shove
on a basketball court rainshowered in glass.
They're in a war, their quick bodies like forcefields
   of mighty male energy
   colliding against each other, trying to steal the ball
   and score.

~

The reverend, the pastor Bishop Arthur Ward,
   who's 74 years old with eyes hidden under
a cloak of eyelids thick and heavy as the long,
   imponderable years,
wipes his forehead with a towel and he whispers a prayer
of deliverance for the Pistons who are in the semi-finals.
And his assistant, a squat man, belly unfolded
   over a belt and munching a hamburger
as if it were a prayer with mustard and ketchup
   spilled on it, and spilling too, over his thick fingers,
nods and chews a yes forward.

~

And then the pastor, crossing his long slender leg
   like a large bird leg over the other one, tells me in a slow drawl
thick as southern molasses and love
that the 'hand that seizes us all' will have us all
   slowly,
like the incessant creep of a blind man
   feeling his way forward through a poorly lit room,

~

and that 'peace starts first in the mind –'

and the assistant, sitting on a wooden stool
   beside us
nods slowly, his neck all gears and agreement,

~

'but you can't have it, this peace –'

the pastor adds backhandedly,
his old eyes scolding back a flurry of other,
   possible thoughts and memories
once I ask him about things like the race riots
   and the wars of this city smoldering
   in ruins, and of factory jobs lost,
and of the one America eating the other America
   up by the hind tail, so that the older one
is unrecognizable any more –

90

'you can't have it once it's on the battlefield –'
and I nod *yes,* here –

                    ~

'because you're *caught,*' he says, accentuating
   the word caught like it's a pick axe
'and it divides you,' he adds
'from both this side and that; and you're cut in two halves,
   like that burned house across from us;
and you never get right with each other
or the street you and your people were born
      on –'

And he waves his hand, a dark, sweeping gesture
   across the ruined home that must resemble
   the world he knows and lives in across the street from us,
like he's giving it a blessing, or some
   final admonishment.

                    ~

Now there's a woman who brings us our plates.
And the boys clash on with their basketball game,
oblivious to the charcoal smells of hot dogs
   and hamburgers, cooking in rows on the grill.
Then we sit in quiet, he and I
   and his assistant,
letting these words sink like food, into our
   common souls.

Fire

To understand how the spirit of the spirit moves
the boy sets an abandoned house on fire.
This is in 1984, during the Devil's Night Fires epoch.
Later, watching the feverish flames awaken
in a bright violent orange, in a devil's night blue,
he thinks he sees his deranged grandfather –
drunk again following his shift at American Axle –
escaping the inferno like a straw broom on fire
and running right through the detonating front window
just like a firestorm of excited, drunken grain liquor.
I watched the boy run after the straw broom on fire,
calling it by name. Later, calling it *I Am*. And to understand
the spirit of the spirit – how it moves into suspense
and into holy mutation – the teenaged girl does tricks
in a wig on Belle Isle, and, pissed off, fired up, she cuts up
a john with a razor blade just to demonstrate to
the both of them what transience feels like, after being
cut open in blood. And to understand the spirit
of the spirit – years earlier – and how it creates change
by harvesting into it an inner glow of concentration –
the radical, who's now sitting intently in a chair
on Grand Boulevard and studying a lonesome bee
trapped in a dusty front window, he, the radical one,
years back, curled in his right hand a pipe bomb and he
hurled it first at a taxi cab and then he hurled
another fire bomb right through the glass windows
of a storefront and, dazed by the glass exploding
he fell backwards, stunned, utterly stunned, and he saw
the hapless inferno angels sent down here by God
just staggering and fumbling prayerfully across 12th Street,
their halos ablaze as one by one they were hit
and they were rolled flat by fast moving vehicles
raging over them. And to study the spirit of the spirit
and how it moves quietly up the charged spine
of flames and cauterizes ideas into physical things –
into heaven and hell pressing up against each other

like competing brothers insisting who'll be right,
who'll set the record straight about Eden being a fire city
and not just a paradise – I watched a man, me, light
a match to fire and I heard me say, praise be to
the fires here. Rage and creation will be burned here
until the *it* returns, the being whose name is *prophecy*:
the one making the physical here so infinite again.

Scrap Metal Mantra
— At the Packard Junkyard, Piquette Avenue, dawn

Holy Hosanna according to the Packards,
        according to the See Murgh Holy Bird
                lighting the leafless shrubs

on this winter morning
        here in this junkyard
                on Piquette Avenue

singing all the wonders
        of the broken down engine world
                in every language,

singing the seven spirits of God
        rising up in fleeting wingspan
                from the bow and quiver

of aluminum fencing —
        in Note of Hand, in nugget of gold,
                in fragrant nucta,

oh miraculous drop of nectar that saves
        a world from the nurr and spell of darkness
                where all that falls

falls wayside in dreary forfeit, in gelid frill,
        in nuncupative will,
                oh holy hosanna of the winter sun

dawning here before me as I straddle
        the seven known Packards
                that could save a city

from sad-bread, from sorrow,
        from scavenger's daughter,
                oh come raise in number

our fortune-coming,
        oh muster of peacocks through weeds,
                oh cluster of wild grapes, nuts and seeds

turned to amber gold of morning sunrise
        rising over slaughter house, over clump of trees,
                over covey of game birds

exploding out of bricks, oh bevy of roes,
        of quails, of larks, of pheasants,
                of the wandering federation

of the unemployed, oh light of the harem,
        oh legion of dogs, whelps,
                foul fiends in fetid suits of clothing

limping through empty hotel rooms and parlors,
        from abandoned shoals
                of mackerel-colored cars

in lazy procession through ghost-dawn haze,
        oh rabble of men
                in ill-fitting clothes,

come sing with the birds and me
        the scrap metal mantra
                waking up the dawn.

Scrappers
– For Jeff Alfier & Tobi Alfier

One by one they arrive in parkas, the vans idling behind them,
and a pit fire singeing the autumn night with aggressive flames,

and an exhausted, dissected building looming beyond them –
an empty glass factory rotting from too much after moisture

and years of squatters, looting and neglect. Its roof opened up,
green tree tops swimming into nighttime stars, and feral dogs

biting the mist as they skulk low, growling into tangled scrap dens
as the intruders scoot them away with high powered water guns

while other men sling rope, and drag the scrap metal and copper
out of the building like torn arteries from a body lying unconscious.

They've come here from the east side and the west, from all parts
of the city where the hunger bites hardest, some of them young,

some with wallets full of baby pictures, some from Kentucky,
some old and drunk, and already worn out, mouths stuffed

with cigarettes and slogans, some like Lewis & Clark on expedition.
All of them canvassing for gold, for the riches of the after burn –

as if the buildings of the city were really just the remaining ruins
of a long ago grounded ship lying beached, its death giving wealth.

And one of the men rips out taut steel, hoists it up in his hands,
as if he's discovered royal gold in an abandoned tomb or palace.

And another, his eyes manic, expressive as owls in darkness,
stampedes out of the rooms of the factory, as if he's found life.

The Burnt Out Prodigals of the Train Station

Under the gaping arches they come,
          parading themselves
                    in fingerless gloves.

Fables of the deconstruction, dust bites
          in the blood of my eyes.
                    Someone calls them

broken bicycles, shelved garbage, leakage.
          The newspapers call them
                    beat angels, refuse muck,

pickers, stealers. One is an enchanter,
          a holy sepulcher of greasy splurge.
                    A Psalmist.

Teeth the color of used up endpaper,
          eyes like fuel,
                    skin burnt as diesel.

One is an empty chance.
          A one time poet. A drunk,
                    a street minister.

One hawks up a saxophone,
          father thoughtful squawking 'Trane,
                    squawking all the fat in the fire,

all the coal in the blaze, spits music.
          Chimney sweep in the ash-grime
                    of a burnt out Cadillac.

Now Gribaldi in a top hat
          bows speculatively,
                    garbles a drink,

bows again to a fire hydrant.
   And Frankie,
     one of the druidic *Ellyllon*

who squats on the outer rim of a fire,
   cobbles out, spits, spats,
     disgusted,

chews on the old smoke in his teeth,
   hurrays and hoo-hahs the dawn,
     chirping birds in his brain,

fire ants in his pants
   as he opens his trousers
     to wiggle dwiddle…

spills his fortune into the weeds.
   I come upon them, here in the grass
     of Roosevelt Park

in front of the train station, fighting kings
   who ignore the economy,
     refuse advice,

refuse love, refuse me,
   refuse all the state-funded
     improvement going on.

They're fathers, really,
   of the Church of
     "Only the Burnt Out Prodigals Remain..."

And we owe them
   for absorbing our nightmares.
     They are our speakeasy Philistines,

our best public housing symbols and signs.
   They remain a delirious
     encomium of ribald drunks

hollering out praises to the morning,
　　　　to the dereliction of duty.
　　　　　　　One of them bends over,

hurls, flays the fox into a card board box,
　　　　raises his roughed-up head
　　　　　　　and he coughs up

last night's drink like a drunken Friar John.
　　　　Raises his head to the Fair Maid
　　　　　　　of February morning

blossoming up through the foul,
　　　　false ceiling of skyline clouds, the sun.
　　　　　　　Then they ramble on

in a rain-tree group through the forecastle
　　　　of ruined cars,
　　　　　　　through open fields

and speckled scrap yards, rumblefish men,
　　　　godless men struck with falling sickness,
　　　　　　　memory, delirious fantigue –

on through the filibuster of traffic,
　　　　through the fill-dyke snow.
　　　　　　　Flat-fish dumbbells they are,

corduroy coat minstrels,
　　　　pop-n-jay fools
　　　　　　　walking yesteryear off.

Like flap dragons,
　　　　our seed oracles, our fortune tellers,
　　　　　　　our kin.

Great Days

The great days are gone here,
says the man drinking with me
here at this bar in the slaughter
house district of Detroit.
Everything is a count down
to indifference now. Even
the cows, their big eyes, pale
and glossed over like drugged
angels before they're butchered
feel it, this indifference,
this countdown to the end
of something, this last act.
Even the butchers, those that
cut the meat that feeds this city
can feel it as they raise a toast
to something lost in themselves
here in these streets that run
like ale away from the city core.
They talk of great days before
these days, where you could
throw all your heart's hopes
on tomorrow, the day after,
when this town was a workman's
dream, a place to get married.
Days where machinery ruled us.
Where music, blues and jazz
at the clubs off the boulevard
turned upside down, sideways,
and you could grab a stranger,
a woman by the loose arm
and dance with her and still
feel respectable. I'm here
too, with them all, drinking,
north of where Strohs used to be.
We're at Bert's Warehouse.
It's afternoon on Russell Street

and the gray wind shuffles
across the lots, spilling papers.
More butchers, drunk, pile in,
the blood still pink on their
fingers, cigarettes lit up
and suspenders caked in red.
They talk about no raises,
how it is a woman can't love
them until they bring home
a paycheck that buys a ring.
No raises worth a ring now.
They talk about necks, livers,
and the way an animal will
stare at you before you cut it,
sort of like a dead man walking.
The sticky stuff in between
ribs, and how it is cutting is a form
of consecration, something in it
that makes aggression feel ok,
especially when you can't
count on what tomorrow brings.
Can't talk about it with a woman.
They shout about that time
last winter when *Cattleman's*
closed, shut down and fired
everybody on the spot with no pay,
and how it is two men left
there, took their rage to Bert's
and clubbed each other,
beer mugs in hand, spilling
ale out on the street because
they were ashamed, stupid.
Useless to someone faceless,
hidden away in another building.
Impotent as those dumb cows
they'd killed a day earlier.
Now daylight darkens, suddenly.
Clouds spread over the smoke
towers of the slaughter house,

and the sea gulls rise south
to the river. And then rain,
a sudden, quick explosion of it,
falls and pelts the streets black,
sweeps all the blood stains away.

St. Catherine of Genoa, at the Rinaldo Arms Manor
–The discovery of Purgatory

She was peeking out of a window in her dark gown, embracing her Crucifix,
her Holy Bible nearby, her writing pad and ink pen, her glass of cool water,
her round little corner table with a green cloth on it, snow, lightly falling,
a sprinkling of Heaven's crystalline debris, while the damned, the junkies,
the prostitutes lining the streets beneath her, those lost souls being found now
with the will to sin, infidels to God's will, were slipping further
and further out of relation with God Almighty – *she could see the light of their souls
blinking on & off &she could watch them flickering, as if full of red rusty dust* –and
becoming part of the unholy, part of the cursed and the damned.

Down the hallway, a woman playing the piano paused, pounded, set forth her
rage against something while Catherine, childless, sterile now as a woman
bathed in salt, in pure alcohol and light, prayed for the sick, the ill, the
childless, the victims of adultery; for unfaithful men holding onto their
genitalia as ornamentation, as wands of black magic, as evil totems,
mis-creations of Christ (whose genitals were of the microcosm of pure elated
creation, of Genesis.) Now her telephone rang, and bent as an old crabstick,
she hobbled over, took it, misunderstood the fast-talking
sales pitch, gently touched the phone down, as if petting a lame goat,
and hobbled back to her Holy Bible, to her ink pen and her writing pad.

Out doors a police situation. Catherine, seeing this, shivered, saw the tree
inside of a man grow suddenly orange, catch flame, become possessed
by Satan as the policeman hand-cuffed him, stuffed him into the car.
Now, light of snow on the sidewalk, she could see the edge of the world
bordering the edge of something utterly faithful, some region where
lost souls, those lining the street outside of the drug store and the porn
book store could not discern that it was there. Calling out, at first to the Book
and the Crucifix, she asked for love of Christ to guide her visions,
to extend her eyes beyond the realms of glamour, so that she could link
with God's Holy vision, his eyes, the mount of his words in the Holy Book.

Soon, dusk, she could envision rusted souls rising like toxic waste
from the sidewalk, could see through the hotel windows men and women
dying, their bodies decomposing, could see the Holy Soul while still
in the flesh, rising, being cradled, held like a rusty pear, and then banished
either down the sewers to Hell, or to this land, this purgatory, this
diachrony of time's figment, this purging of sin by fire, by absence
from the most holy, to this place where souls would kneel for their rising.

She could see that these souls, these crepuscules of light stained by sin,
by sinfulness, would be lifted up, be harbored there, and retain no memory
of this upon their shock of first arrival, for that would mean the stealing
of a private memory from *God*, and thus there could be no memory that
He did not see.

And so she wrote of this: wrote by hand well into the night, well past
the embolism of falling snow, well past the diabetic glow of street lamps
and the crewelwork of windows encasing her in. For she was a shut in –
she was just a small crista of God's mitochondria, his sacred experiment
of assimilation into the Divine. And as dawn bled across the white snow,
bled through the heating towers, stained the rick-a-shaw of debris
scattered and urinated on along the abandoned fields of the city, and bled
through the shuttered homes – those correlatives of Godless men without
eyes wide awake and seeking Heaven and its structures of light, its light
on endless light – she could see this work, this *treatise*, was of God's
word. It was his blessing for the souls wanting in. For those wanting
to ferry across the Holy Fire, St. Elmo's fire, and join together
with God in rapture.

It was for those here in the broken-down city that would be baptized
and join the Corposant, the Holy Body of the Divine, like her. And travel
from the injured corners of the city, its Racism and its Purgatory, and cross
the veils of forgetting and lift their aching bodies over the broken river
to Paradise, with her. Though she couldn't leave yet, for she was gravely ill,
she still had spiritual work to do here and the dawning light was touching
her injured leg. It was empurpling her arthritis. She was someone's great
aunt, waiting for the morning. Her stomach was growling. And I could
hear her moving up there. I could hear her up in her apartment, shuffling
across the kitchen floor, making her coffee. She was having the rapturous
visions of St. Catherine of Genoa, that *seer*, that missionary of the Divine
who discovered the pure light of Purgatory – I could hear her up there
at her black stove, making her coffee, notating in her Bible, praying for me.

104

An Elegy for Deletha
A Black woman plunges to her death in the Detroit River
as a crowd of onlookers stands idly by as she is attacked

When that man threatened you with a metal pipe,
you jumped into the waterknotted filth of the dark,
Detroit River. And thrashing your arms, stringy
now, and as spread out as loose cheese, you were sucked
under in the undertow, a goner, and your clumsy
body must have surfaced and sank, your head
bobbing above the angry rippling currents, your gasps
of breath strained and unheard, your throat taking on water.
I think your helpless legs must have been kicking
wildly like a duck until at last you grew tired, exhausted,
and the weeds below tangled with your weak shoe laces,
and then you slipped under, a victim, just a part
of the refuse caught like fatigued debris in the river.
It's alright, Deletha, because we all live sinfully;
and we all strip down to summer clothes in a place
where beauty's a doomed romance. You were high too,
on PCP, which is a strange way to spend your
last night alive on this earth. And like most who drown,
lost in the car wreckage of their plans and excuses, you,
too, were looking for true love in all the wrong places,
and you found a man who could finally give you
what you didn't want to deserve, which must have been
violence or an accident, or murder, who really knows
what we invite into the stagecraft of our lives. And when I
dream of you, floating aimlessly through the black evening
before you went under, I think of you watching Belle Isle
with its throngs of bright cars all crowded together
on the bridge getting smokier and smaller. The island lights,
flickering, and all the words in your head getting numbed.
Deletha, I wonder if everyone gets their gravestone
blessed once for their existence in this life? Even you?
I wonder if you got blessed? And I wonder, sitting here
in this friendly café and sipping my coffee with this child,
who's just about twelve years old, and her eyes as alert
as a horse's eyes when they look at me over the table

waiting for the cold soda that will solve all that thirst
behind her big, elaborate teeth, whether your eyes,
dulled, and the color of grit and ash, were awake
when your soul passed the Renaissance Center and its lights
on your defeated journey to Wyandotte. And I wonder
if you had a father or a mother who'd buy you cold soda,
later, when the storms of the middle summer took over,
sheared the small fragile leaves from the drenched trees,
and the hard rains pelted this sad, disordered life we live in
before you were drowned in the river. And also, I wonder
whether the waves, bouncing in the gray, polluted wind,
kept your shoulders afloat for an hour, before your two hands,
like limp hubcaps, like angels of recitation, went under.

I Want to Tell You
– At the Abandoned Packard Plant

I want to tell you that I drove there, to the Packard Plant,
    a veteran of a war
Camouflaged behind weeds and fallen debris
Like a demolished barracks from another era
    where fine men, through sweat and bruises, made new Packard cars
For a future and a promise, on East Grand Boulevard
    at Mt. Elliott,
And where a motel and a neighborhood of damaged lives
    go nowhere.
                    ~
It was raining, early in May, and I had to halt for a long,
Patient funeral procession snaking its way into Trinity Cemetery.
                    ~
After the line of cars completed, I turned right
    on East Grand Boulevard. And up
The street, past open fields full of barrels holding waste
    the old Plant, muffled in decay, sat there in the gray rain,
Collecting the dark moldiness of rain splattered buildings.
    On the sidewalk to my left there was a homeless man
Strutting past the plant. He was punching at the government
    of psychosis and yelling out
Long unhappy sermons to the open windows.
                    ~
Down the street, just beyond the plant, the Packard Motel's
    parking lot was full, and a brown dog was sniffing weeds.
I remember talking to a priest, he was gentle, and he told me
    hookers took tricks there, to the old motel
Sitting there in the shadow of the ruined plant,
    and they traded sex for crack, the usual currency.
And he told me that people make love with what they believe in.
On the top of their hand is a "name," in the palm a "wish,"
    and what they clutch in their fist *conceives them*,
    which is how people in a relationship make love.

Which made me think of old scenes from the Bible
   and the way relationship is like an assembly plant,
A factory, creating everything sacred to it, and so is a city,
   and he gently nodded at me, passed me my book,
Slowly closed the shutters on the church rectory windows.
                              ~

I could have told him death was holding court here,
   at the cemetery and at the old mangled plant,
And at the motel where a dark-skinned woman
Was making cheap love to one of her tricks
While the overhead light bulb sizzled a ray of gold
   onto the dilapidated bed,
And that even the sunlight was tinged with a funeral pallor,
Especially in the May rainfall spilling over graves
   and across the car-clogged city streets.
                              ~

I could have told him that laughter and forgetting
Are the bitter pills of the lamented and the lost,
And of those forgotten by opportunity, grandeur and time,
   but he wouldn't have listened or cared.
And that's because he knew better the ruined smoke
Of fire and ash getting stuck in peoples' throats,
And so anything they say becomes a raging spit ball of fire.
                              ~

And I knew too, that peoples' thoughts were twisting –
   like broken car fenders into a kind of rage and hatred,
Because the air outside was flushed with anger,
   but that on the inside of the palm, always,
Is the spectacular force of forgiveness and love.

Inamorata
– Romance of the Spirit of Detroit Statue & the Passo di Danza Statue

Sunset
and
the stars
over
the river,
ardent,
impassioned,
he,
the spirit
of the city
holding in hand
a rotating planet,
a bronze ball
of needlepoint
rocket flame
leaping out
to pierce
the night,
to fill it
with
erotic
tenderness,
and in his
other
hand,
in his
palm
a group
of people
rising up,
a noah's arc
of singers
singing
a capella,
and down street
from him

a nude,
raising
her lullaby
arms up
to uncoil
her hair
and let it
down
under
the glow
of the
moon,
oh
passo
di danza
paramour
dancer
he breathes
to himself,
oh lover
bathing
under glow
of
the stars
in front
of
the gas
company,
step
down street
to greet me,
oh
sweet
libertine
lover,
dance me
to joy.

At the Blue Diamond Lounge

Soft glow of dancers patrolling the dance floor with each other,
flaunt and gallop of busty girls in two step, in mambo-tango and men

in full cowboy hats, cowhide boots, jewel studded belts, mustaches,
melt and jump of glitzy women leaping up into men's upheld arms

in jolt and frenzy, in twist and twirl, in lyrical circus, in stiffened
celebration as the Mexican Accordion Band parades the tango

forward through exuberant citrus frolic, through harlequin dovetail
furrow as we sip our tequila, here on Campbell Street at Vernor,

Christmas lights of Mexican Town flamboyant, glowing men and girls
in rows at Duly's eating coney dogs at 2 am, Manny collecting pay.

Jesus of the Scrap Yards

I see him raising heaven amidst the scrap metal.
Watch him, a robed man in unruly beard, summoning
all the dead scrap metal here to rise up from the dead,
to be lifted up, to be glorified. See him shuffling through
the heaps of scrap wood and ashes, scuffling through
the long, sharp-edged strands of aluminum siding,
watch him kicking the *Gloria in Excelsis* all throughout
the scrap yard with his boots, his vagabond leprosy,
his soiled, broken English, grave digger that he is
whose soul, full of mad rapture, is the forty hours
devotion, the mercury prayer, the scrap metal mantra,
calling all the ruin here to rise up again, recycled.
I watch him raise the strips of metal in his charcoal hands,
watch him give it all back to heaven, to its birth right,
to the god of metal, Hephaestus, as the junk yard dogs,
unleashed from their hatches by the guard sheds,
lunge out at him, rip at his tattered coat rags. I hear
him calling out madly – Jesus of the Scrap Yards,
bleak skin, gray as the March sky, eyes bulging out,
broken-throated, with a voice of graveled charcoal –
rise up oh metal of the scrap yards to the soot sky:
rise up again to the *Gloria in Excelsis* of production,
oh Creed of Detroit City.

Detroit Hymnal

The hymn was ensnared inside the chickadee's beak.
I could hear the hymn choked in there. Startled almost.

This was outside of a 57' Packard, in a junk yard
on Piquette Avenue. On an autumn day in Detroit.

The sky penetrated by strange clouds. Bulged with snow.
The chickadee passed from each tangled branch.

Crooked its head. Dared me to sing a hymn back to it.
After the hymnal burns the song returns as a fruit.

~

Praise is one of the heart's holy hymnals, isn't it?
God said, Detroit will be one of the lonely purple gray hymns at dusk.
Dense with songs and praise, with holy reparatory to God.

Wracked with entangled fences. Dense with fruits and berries.
Lost automobile thrones loud with hurdy-gurdy singing birds.

I will find myself tangled in silence amongst Packards.
My heart a strange fruit. A hymnal choked there inside it.

The chickadee parachuted through tangled gray branches.
A hiding hopeful note. Its wings getting lost or found in dark.

Smoke burst from a chimney stack across the field.
I sat there listening to it for all I was worth.

~

You are a hymnal too, I said aloud to myself.
A scrap metal mantra. Beauty inside rust.

A bruised berry. A throat choked with birds.
Fruit exploding. A melodious songbird light.

Letter to ML Liebler, from La Salle Boulevard

ML: I'm writing to you from La Salle Boulevard,
near Hitsville, USA. I've just had steaming coffee.

I've explored the Modus Vivendi of 12th Street
beyond La Salle Boulevard & Clairmont Street

where some sort of sustained peace was forged –
be it in hot flames or in apathy, perhaps in love.

ML, this city's music is about power & glory –
& the way it renders all our conflicted feelings

into a greater apotheosis of oneness. We feel it deep
inside our dance floor bodies, all gyrating together

to the Detroit Hustle, & it takes us right on into
the Sacred Divine that's on fire inside us as we dance.

My brother, this is the bold truth we all believe in.
Every one of us, punching knobs on a hot juke box.

Every one of us, swinging at Bert's Market Place,
PJ's Lager House, The El Club, St. Andrews, Harpos.

William James, exasperated, said, "*people want war*,"
& Marvin, his eyes elevated to the gray skies sang

to us, "you know we've got to find a way to bring
some loving here today," & William Blake, earlier,

declared that it's best that we try, in fact, to find the
true war: "*Wars of love*." Music – its energy – brings

upheaval. From torment into conflict, from lust &
passion, we've *all* been consumed in the sacred fires

of this city's wild guitars, its bass lines, its drum rolls.
ML, Detroit's wild music — from the grief-stricken

pleadings of its vocalists standing delirious & readied
at their microphones & pressing on for a greater love

& peace — has shown us we're made of two cities:
body & *soul*. & in those two cities, we're the psychic

streams of the volatile & the peaceful, flowing as one.
Maybe Sartre's always been right: *love is violence*…

(The MC5 at Tartar Field, blasting away the apathy
until the music, ripped from rebellious rage, ignited.

The Four Tops, leaning into the heartache of illusion,
bellowing out, "darling reach out… I'll be there with

a love that will see you through")…yea, that's it —
that's the scripture we're here together to witness:

Love's a redemptive gift of upheaval; it's made from heat
& a passionate hope. I fall into me, believing all this.

ML, I could continue confessing to you these truths:
the way we hang our heads, alone now, afraid.

How we cling together at the dance parties or at the
after-hours clubs, mouthing what music's made of:

these lyrical pearls scribed on page while musical notes
erupt together, in the mythical body called Detroit.

(Smokey Robinson leaning into the microphone
at Hitsville USA, the musicians pulsing behind him,

bellowing out the lyric, "so if you feel like giving me
a lifetime of devotion, I second that emotion.") ML,

115

I think Smokey's lyric gets it right: that if we live it,
this notion to love a future better, *I second the emotion.*

The diversity of our conscious tongues all singing high
into the night's inflection of moon & stars & hope.

Walking up La Salle Boulevard, behind the kid
who's riffing his rip rap through head phones –

his swagger made of muscled rust & true belief,
his eyes lit in prayer – I can't believe it any better.

The Flautists at the Michigan Central Train Depot

were all playing the flute together in a small prayer circle
     in Roosevelt Park
          where the abandoned train station

stood silent and still in the foggy heaving
     of the morning's first sunlight,
          and the stumble bums, drunk,

had collapsed like ragged beat angels
     underneath the milky way of trees to listen.
          It was autumn, the heart-closing time

where the last murmuring of summer
     turns a heel and scatters all the lonesome people
          without a roof to winter,

and the falling leaves whirled one by one to wither.
     The prayer group of young flautists –
          all of them just out of their teens

and mixed together in pairs – practiced opening
     the oldest and deepest known threshold
          of heaven with each other.

This was in the end times,
     following the zero-energy-condition
          after the last war in this city

where the emergence from nothingness held sway.
     A shiny Plymouth Fury
          was parked along Michigan Avenue,

its driver, a mystery, because time here in the city
     had come to a stand still,
          and none of us knew whether it was

the after-burn of the riots, or perhaps
        time had moved laterally
                and we were into the future.

The group of flautists were gathered here
        to awaken and bless the collapsed voice
                of we the people who had fallen

in the Pompeii inferno, the *67' riots* and everything thereafter,
        which would then open the gates
                to the *resurrection*, or perhaps

it would become the musical insurrection
        of the jazz-infused flute, the heart's slithering tongue.
                Their leader,

the reincarnated molecular impression
        of Yusef Lateef – that impassioned
                virtuoso of riotous music –

had stirred to electrified life the song *Woodward Avenue*.
        He stood there, rallying and vaulting the notes
                as if recovering something silver

from his own fire-burned throat,
        and he softly instructed
                one of his youngest players,

a woman with eyes as wide as a woodland vole
        who was wrapped in red scarves
                and a furry brown coat,

that the flute should coax back to *whistled livingness*
        the spiraled arc of our anguished voices,
                all our souls, rising out of the flames.

At Better Made Potato Chips, Gratiot Avenue, Detroit

I see him flogging the dead horse of the morning in deluged
      pantomime, this street corner traveling salesman preaching

how the hole in the belly will be healed in the mouths of those
      taking to tongue these "made in Detroit" potato chips

deep fried and sold here in the midst of the neighborhood,
      here, at the corner of Gratiot and Georgia Streets,

where the fresh salty smell is rising Heavenward
      in a yellow skein of seasoned aromatic sizzle

over the Edsel Ford Freeway from the bulging release vents
      of the Better Made Potato Chips Factory.

This is at eight in the morning, where the salt shimmering haze
      of food production, wafting across the derelict flummery

of broken homes and the limbus partum of broken down cars,
      mixes together with drunks coming home from the bars.

Something about the Florentine oval of potato chip wedges
      and their translucent Heaven-made taste

coupled with the idea of Detroit feeding me a morning kiss
      from her home-made, fresh salty mouth,

compels me to stop my car and purchase a bag for myself,
      oh sweet brine of salt-stinging sin on my tongue,

oh sweet angel wing of the morning's yellow-bagged crunch,
      Oh sweet summertime drug.

Automotive Wedding, Packard Junkyard, Piquette Avenue

I kissed you in a swarm of abandoned Packards.
Heard a junkyard quartet of noisy sparrows

and grackles greeting us as we entered the church
of suspension frames and rusted transmissions.

The best man and the maid of honor stood at attention
outside a 71' Gran Torino. Walked in front of us

along a path of chrome bumpers till we stood
there in front of the reverend who held a car manual.

We were married there among the feral cats.
Said vows full of factory rhetoric. He married us

among a noisy tangle of twisted rose briar shrubs
underneath a sloping archway of leafy witch hazel.

We crawled in and out of dusty back seats to find out
where we belong. Found our fortune on our hands and knees

looking for your wedding ring among steering columns
and rusted tire rims. Found the way to Heaven

stretching our bare legs out together in the vinyl seats
watching the drive-in movie of stars and lightning

rising over the Fisher Plant and Detroit Stamping.
Grilled our wedding dinner in a fire pit outside

the swinging door of a 55' Packard for wind shelter.
Made love together to the morning traffic's roar.

Friday Night in Excelsis (Detroit)
– For Tim Murad

Young women sitting in chairs
        outside Café D' Mongo,
               and men in tight jeans,

slender hands
        holding onto cigarettes,
               glasses of whiskey,

the whole street ablaze
        with chatter,
               with happy

scuttlebutt and celebratory vibrato,
        talk of Astro Coffee
               in Corktown,

ribs at Slows BBQ
        on Michigan Avenue,
               and new condos

erected in Midtown,
        the man at the piano
               inside playing Chopin

if you can believe it,
        his silver hands
               sliding across piano keys

in quick, sexual strokes,
        his eyes closed tightly,
               all the subdued anger

in them gone,
        rattlesnake bite of racism
               evaporated,

white and black folks playing chess
        inside together,
                and at the Cobra Strip Club

across from us,
        here on Griswold,
                it's noisy, but empty,

because everyone's gathered here
        to party,
                to rediscover the city,

to take in the embellishments
        of summer,
                the holy hosanna

of one rustbelt city
        coming back to *love* again,
                one piano key at a time,

brother to brother,
        sister to sister,
                man to man

and lover with lover, arm in arm,
        wrists extended
                around waists,

races mixed with races,
        a glorious real estate
                of possibility,

an assembly line
        full of noises, full of laughter,
                full of hope.

The Girls at the Vista Maria Home for Truants

We wait here, standing among the trees
    losing all their leaves.
        The runaway girls gather at the windows

in intimate pairs. The blonde with the hoop earrings huddles
    against the raised shoulders
        of the freckle-faced girl

stretched tight in her silver mini skirt and her tank top,
    and the brunette in fishnet stockings
        and the scar across her left cheek

nudges against the Latino girl with the crucifix tattoo
    stippled across her left wrist.
        And just for a flickering moment,

like sparkling fish that volley and swarm
    and then heave against the rock walls
        to get a better spot in the crowded throng,

the girls push back and forth together
    like eager fans at a concert.
        And they heave and sigh

and they release their waiting emotions again…
    We teenage boys, who stand outside the windows,
        tease and taunt them.

We gaze in through the cracked window panes,
    hungry eyes.
        Make gestures at the girls

to break free, come run away with us.
    We fall back together, sip our open beers
        at the side door of the 71' Gran Torino.

Later on, whispering to one of the girls
        who kneels down to blow cigarette smoke at us
                through a crack in the window pane,

along the ledge where the laundry room dryers
        whirl and burl with the swish and roll
                of drying bed sheets,

I run my fingers across the edge of glass there,
        and I touch her thin finger,
                our hands, merciful strangers,

finding flame.

Watching Bilal Fall

Because in the Arabic, the name *Bilal, or Billy,*
      when spoken in its native
            Middle Eastern tongue,

means, "The Chosen One,"
            we watch Bilal fall.
                He *is* falling –

like a zodiac of chosen twilight
         from a dilapidated window
             high up in The Brewster Projects.

He has been rousted
        from his reverie –
             during his deep contemplation

of the city nudging her silver face
        through a wedding veil of clouds for him to kiss,
            by four who wish to rob him –

right here, beneath the starlight as he skateboards
        across an abandoned basketball court
            bathed in sunset,

and he's been shot in the face
        with a pistol and then laid out flat
            in a bed of weeds and debris,

even though he can barely
        speak English,
            and even though the money

he's carrying in his wallet will later be spent
        on fast food and weed.
            And even as he is expiring,

he knows that all who vanish must at first
		rise up –
				like a flame climbing up

a twisted tree branch –
		and so he rises up
				to the highest tower

of these vacant Brewster Projects,
		to fall.
				And so we watch

his elongated, slender body
		spiraling downward,
				into wood piles and bindweed.

He is aiming himself down like a squid,
		into the ribboned twist and swirl
				of chaos.

Isn't this what the artist studies –
		the unpredictable twist
				and swirl of chaos?

Isn't this what we volunteer to marry –
		alchemists in artistry –
				even at the time of dying?

And so he falls like a squid
		freeing himself
				from the familiar

aurora of nerves and lather –
		from the lock-up of his bone structure –
				like he is still within the instant,

even now, because the wonder
		of this experience
				is too aerial for him to miss.

And like all who have been chosen
    to resemble a star
        unveiling its five-pointedness

from birth robe to jaw bone
    to white glissando matter,
        we watch him demonstrate

his falling – through the air like a super nova –
    into this cradle of plank wood,
        lying there like his coffin.

It's not the city's fault, you say –
    she was only the new bride in his eyes
        because he'd blessed her that way.

It's not the killers' fault, nor the projects,
    for they were simply there
        to teach the meaning of how we are chosen.

And because he is the chosen one
    we watch him
        open his giant squid eyes

like a deep water diver
    as he drives his gaze
        into the grid arteries of the savage city.

And he spins and he needles in –
    freeing himself of all matter,
        into his next graffiti splatter.

And from his mouth come the words,
    "I'm savagely wild. *I am…*"
        This is how I am chosen.

1981, Revisited
— 457 East Kirby, Detroit

It's the year the president is shot.
By John Hinkley on a mission to
impress Jody Foster — who's some-
thing less than 25 and couldn't
care less. Is probably sick to her
stomach later that night. The scene
outside the Washington Hilton is
frenetic. I'm at a bank getting cash out.
My apartment's been robbed. We
think it's the drug pushers downstairs.
I'm hiding my cash in a vent.
I'm dating a med student but she's
scared shitless of the Cass Corridor.
She'd rather dig through a rib cage.
She's jumpy every time we kiss and
the drug dealers start threatening war.
I hear the event on the radio, at a
drive through. That's after tuning
past The Talking Heads *More Songs
About Buildings & Food.* The day's
a crabby, gray version of winter taking off,
Spring time about to happen.
There are small sparrows chirping
like mad in a flowering cherry tree.
There's girls trying on spring purses.
This is long before I hold a kid
on my lap and whisper I love you,
and I learn that girls need fathers who
will tell them over & over again
that they are special and oh so brave,
and she kisses my cheek. It's long
before there is pandemonium in the sky.
Nobody like Billy Ray Cyrus exists.
MTV is the rage on TV. You see British
punk bands mixing with American.
You see bands you'll never see again.

Charles & Diana marry at St. Paul's
in London, and it's fairy tales. Nobody
paying attention to Di's eating habits
or to that Bowles woman Chuck fancied.
That same year there are 2.1 million
divorces, the most ever recorded.
This is years before my marriage.
I'm living in an apt in Detroit, behind
the Art Institute. Steely Dan's *Hey 19*
plays below me all night long at a drug
den and there's an old car parked out-
side on the snowy street with a bumper
sticker that reads, *"Gun Control's Being
Able to Hit Your Target –"* The term ugly
American had been used by a loud-
mouthed but often times accurate radio
talk show caller to refer to Americans,
living abroad, who remain ignorant of
local culture. This is around the time
of the hostage crisis and its resolution.
We all still call the Arabs *camel jockeys*.
It's Spring or Winter. My apartment
is robbed a week earlier and we are
still trying to figure out why John
Lennon has been murdered. The guy
who robbed my apartment is black.
Maybe eighteen years old. I catch him
but he escapes my grip. And he runs to
freedom across a street and into the vast,
impregnable blight of east side Detroit.
Raising his fist as he runs. I'm not sure
if this is a gesture of Black Power,
which makes me think of the words that
Stokely Carmichael said when he said,
*"I'm not going to beg the white man
for anything I deserve. I'm going to take
it."* But who am I to get into big stick
politics. We're all living in the same
filthy circumstances. We're all

129

having the same John Hinkley fantasies.
None of us believe that we will ever
marry an English princess or an
Arabic woman who smells like jasmine.
None of us believe we'll have the luck
to kiss someone as rich as Jody Foster.

Woodward Avenue Elegy

— For Starlene the Stripper & Vincent Chin

The elegy — because it's a broken down dream of Detroit City,
    which is, itself, a long unwavering story
of creation and absence being written and unwritten
    over Woodward Avenue's concrete canvas —
stops here on Peterboro, in Chinatown, just outside
the old Chung's restaurant where I trace with my hands
a mural dedicated to Vincent Chin
    who was killed by two men and a baseball bat, in 1982.
Vincent Chin's face is there, smiling. The soft blues of it
    feel rough on my fingers.
The street's a hodgepodge of broken glass, needles and weeds.
I've driven here just to see the mural. A few hapless junkies
suck on day old bread and toss crumbs to the pigeons.
There's a stripper standing near me and her name is *Starlene*,
    which is a fancy word play on star, or starlit, or starlight-
    star bright, and her face is done up in the old-fashioned way
    that was meant to freshen things up, you know,
    or to remodel things, or to completely wash away the
psychology of unpleasantness, to glamour things up with a flash —
    as if everyone who could dance, you know, deserved *fins* —
although Starlene is draped in a shadowy shawl right now
    and she won't remember me nor anybody else,
    because she's been absorbed, like a fist-full of glittery paint,
into so many other voices yelling against her very presence.

                                ~

Every stripper dances against men's absence.
That's what they're here to do. They dance until something brutal
happens.
This one danced for Vincent Chin. And through her tears,
    there's no enduring love, no semblance of Vincent Chin here...
    just the onlookers watching us. One or two stroke their arms,
    waiting for the quick prick and relief of a needle.
One starts yelling for an act of justice, one shakes a fist at nothing.
I tell you Detroit City is — in fact — a stripper named Starlene.
She's like the poem, *starlight, star bright,*

and she's dancing against men's absence.
Against their failure to know the truth of anything.
The killing happened on Woodward Avenue, in the parking lot
    of a McDonalds fast food joint in Highland Park
where the ramshackle streets and the burnt-out brownstone flats
are trashed, and sullied up with crack-addicted street walkers
and windowless strip clubs. And the old auto plant factories,
south of here and vacated in New Center, sit there howling out
for their past glories. I tell you, nothing in Detroit happens
except for to tell again and again the story of absence.
It reminds me – I'm not kidding – of a story that Starlene
once confided to me
while shoving the wad of kleenex under the black brassiere
    that she was wearing as part of her Cat Woman look
and, the story was that, as she spoke with her male clients
on the 900 line, while chewing peanut butter and celery sticks
    and thumbing absently through a fashion magazine,
that she could actually tell when the men were lighting their
cigarettes because of the momentary *click* –
    and then the air, charmed with hot flame in her imagination,
    made her vanish
because she could sense the men fondling themselves
    while blowing smoke rings, and it made her feel absent,
like she'd been gouged out of something, or never was even *in* it,
which because it was subtle and violent, became violent
    and then quite ordinary as if she could just get used to it,
because it was a part of her morning routine, part of her
    daytime job. *People live in the half-life of what they've done*,
she said. And *what the hell*, she said, it makes them what they are.
                            ~

And violence –
    which fills up the factory line with its own special circumstance –
    turns ordinary people absent, and then it strikes. The killing
happened after Vincent Chin and two out-of-work autoworkers
quarreled over a stripper whose name was *Starlene*,
    dancing there in front of them
at the *Fancy Pants Saloon*, in blighted old Highland Park.
The two white men thought he was Japanese,
and one of the causes for their unemployment, and the older

132

of the two men beat Vincent Chin to death with a baseball bat,
as if trying for a Detroit Tigers two-run triple.

Vincent Chin wasn't Japanese. Truth is he was Chinese-American.
Starlene is whispering all of this to me.
If you saw Vincent's face from Starlene's eyes as she gazed down
at him from her safe spot on the dancing deck, the glittery lights
roaming and polka-dotting across the dark ignorant walls of the club
and the drunken faces blurred, like a mixture of heated flames,
you'd see a large red tumor overtaking his head. I think part
of Vincent's brain was mixed like ketchup
    with fresh gasoline on the road. History, you know, is *bunk* –
this is what Henry Ford, the modern father of this city, said,
and a cop, just out of an argument with his wife about money,
would be scratching his temple, absently too, and pissed off
    at the crime call because of its utter uselessness –
and the horror of its mad insanity and bigotry. And its price –
against the simplicity of an evening of talk radio and donuts.
Christ, he would have said, and Godammit. History is bunk.
Maybe there was a box of French Fries too. And an empty love note
    to the future. Time is bunk, the cop would say.
Time's like a love note to the future and it says: *go away faster.*
It's like gobbling up fast food. It's like strip-dancing in Detroit.
And whatever you do, don't even hide your own steps.
Dance yourself like you'd never stop. Dance across your own name,
    to see to it that it's like a vanishing, chromed and charmed
    advertisement, a bronze plate across your own identity,
and erase history as if it never existed...because history,
    Henry Ford said, is *bunk*: it's a sharp razor blade, this ability
to speed across the highways and cut out all the bad history –
    so that all the new signs cover up all the old signs.
And that's how time – the way we live it here – because it's
the great Model T, the trophy of progress – flies away,
and it shows us that time and history are just a load of bunk.
        So forget about the Goddamn city. *Just forget about it...*
    That's what the cop says, as he scrapes Vincent Chin up.
                        ~
I wonder if Starlene, who was dancing heartbreak
    into 2am and thereafter

133

during the dancing of her usual routine, during Vincent's beating,
and who was busily watching her toes digging into their flirty,
    well-practiced twists and turns,
and who was deliberately grinding the fizzled balls of dust
    beneath her sexy, pearl-studded pumps and then aggressively
    crushing them into tiny little junk yards, into tiny little mass graves
    or little puff balls all rolled up into a pile on the suffocated,
    red marble stage that nobody, really, in the industry gave a shit
about –

I wonder if she could see the small irritated piles of sweet nothings,
    mind you,
the American dream of herself being reduced to pie crust, to rubble –
and I wonder if she could feel what it felt like to crush *everything*
unpleasant,
    and then to reduce it and then just kill it by dancing over it,

because time and history are *bunk*, they are the advertisement –
    the especial out-sourcing of what people do while trying to forget
themselves, while trying to forget their ideals, their nightmares,
their foolish mistakes and transgressions,
    all their losses and gains being pulverized into street trash.

  And I wonder if she was doing it just to snuff out something truly
    deadly she'd been dreaming of all of her life so as to forget it
    or rename it – like one big dancing stage where everything horrid
    could be renegotiated under the cloaked terms of veiled allure
    and seductive advertisement and, as if the stage were – in fact –
    the impregnable city, the renegotiated Sodom and Gomorrah and
    as if the stage was some kind of battle field for every horrid
      anxious thought she'd ever had and could let go of, could just
      erase –
because she'd been wearing her dancer's face, her mask of beauty
    just to get the strength of her face behind it, to forget it all –
so that she could look down too, almost contemptuously, at the
    faces beneath her own, painted glamorous face and feel lucky
    and above it all and pretend to love them anyway because they
    were Detroit Auto workers getting loudly obliterated, drunk
    and ruined, because even *that* history is just bunk…

I wonder if Starlene, who *is* Detroit, and who's dancing her lover's
   dance under a mirror ball, a twirling disco globe, a defeated
industrial God
sees me and Vincent Chin standing here on this side street
shaded with disconsolate old trees and burned-out buildings?
   We're huddled together beneath the low snarl of polluted clouds.
And the sky above us – which is a wrought iron tint at dusk –
is already into its dirty dusty-gray day-glow, its cancerous pedigree.
   And the hallowed-out office towers of rental buildings uptown,
   where we once held our hopes and our dreams inside our hands,
stand around empty and angry like museums of abandonment.

I wonder – as Starlene's just scooped her left arm into mine right
   now – whether she would have felt Vincent's fingers crawling
   up her sleek legs, as if grasping onto the tree of life?
I wonder if she danced fast anyway, flinging him into his Heaven…
Maybe that's what all Detroit strippers do. Maybe that's all any of us
   do.
Maybe that's all we can do. We dance for the celebration of life,
   even if our life – right here and now – is like a faded, sinking star.

Detroit imitates a sinking star. It's like the glorious Titanic,
sinking down into Woodward Avenue. Woodward Avenue –
   which is really what this poem's about –
is a text for logging sinking stars. Everything on it is disappearing –
   into a vast sea of *objet d' art*, of things isolated, torched, replaced.

Everything's changing and being *renamed* to fit the new times we're in.
Even the big old Renaissance Center. Even the dope addicts
   wrapped up in their hoodies with burned-out pistons for eyes.
Even the impoverished prideful poor, those folks being forgotten
   as progress trains on, lacerating everything in its progressive wake.
Even Starlene and her sleek dancer's Cat Woman legs…is vanishing…
She and I stroll to the edge of memory. Vincent Chin's there
   with his two killers. We stand in a group of five.

Woodward Avenue's sizzling with traffic all the way from the

135

stomach – which is the nauseous Detroit River downtown –
to 8 Mile Road where the old main line expands into Ferndale,
Pleasant Ridge, Royal Oak, Berkley and Birmingham.

Nothing else is left for us to celebrate or mourn here, says Starlene,
    bending down to pull off her pumps and undo her lace brassiere
    so she can stretch out on her unmade bed, smoke, and giggle
    quietly while she reads the silver stars – the tarot cards – rising
    up over her lonesome balcony.
There's nothing left to build or to destroy that's not a part of us all
already, she says…our lives are now out-source-able.
And then she lays back, lights a cigarette, sips a cold can of beer
    and says,
We're at the end of the industrial road.

Zombieland
– Park & Sproat Street, Detroit

I wished you a tomb in the dirt.
A place to lay forever undisturbed.
One with a star-shaped flower,
growing up out of mud for you.
Just one flower for your days of eternity.
Something living among the many
who roam here remaining dead,
even though you all hang out here,
zombies, wandering forlorn and lost,
like rotten puppets on a rope
prepping to die, or waiting for your dinner,
either alternative ok by you.
I wished you hammers and valentines.
Blunt objects to kill or love you.
All the types of outcomes due you.
Across the vacant Hotel Eddystone, someone's
scrawled *Zombieland* over its façade.
Was that one of you, emblazoning
your home-sweet-home *nom de plume*
right there, across it, so you all
could mark your nocturnal boldness
as no longer repugnant to the light?
Let me warn you: those who fear you,
will *will* new life here – they'll rip
this penitentiary down, and your home
will be made over, for excited others.
I know you'll stumble away from here.
Perhaps to the burned Temple Hotel?
The haunted Hotel Ansonia on Cass?
You wear hilarity and horror across your faces,
even as you crawl blindly along
the sidewalk, munching day old bread.
Even the feral dogs avoid you.
Maybe you stand upright –
dead in your eternal wakefulness –
waiting for me. I wish I wore

a razor across my face
so that you could see the blades
as they bloody up my lips and mouth
as I chew a smiled farewell to you.

Letter From The New Center District

The noises that I hear – from around the corner
here on Oakland Avenue at Horton Street

where the fisher king of the burn district
shuffles toward me pushing a grocery cart

and firing off impassioned hymns and proclamations
against the facades of store fronts in order to sanctify

the fire from within – are the melody of the district's
magisterial hours. This fellow's a Street Parish Toot.

He's a minister of the House of Fire, The Holy Church
Of The Assembled Gate, The Pillar Of Spire and Ruin.

I can no longer count the assassinations. I can
no longer witness the egg foo young of the sunset

as it slips sideways off the table of daylight to smear
the buildings brown and yellow, cornish hen gray.

The spindly trees darken to the color of brown roux.
The wrecked cars smoke in the dusk's embers.

And the store fronts, half awake with constant eyes,
dim slowly out until the melody of night birds

drips like rice wine from the roof tops and the hand gun
staccato explodes from behind the chestnut trees.

This is the witching hour where the true soldiers
of beat and street rhythm step forth as blood brothers.

The boy on the bicycle riding up Oakland Avenue
to buy milk for his mother wears the roguish face

of a rodent, and skin the color of shredded roast
beef. He's doing his rip-rap. I can no longer confess

for him. He is the seed carrier. The inheritance.
To write this poem for him is to celebrate his fire.

Smoke

"How many losses does it take to stop a heart,
  to lay waste to the vocabularies of desire" – Dorianne Laux

1.

You can see the smokestack curl of it
in the old man's eyes
as he stares back at you from
the soiled chair he's sitting in,
    the small pint of liquor smuggled
down into the cushion
of the chair so you won't
    see it —

his one hand softly patting the cushion like he's trying
    to reveal something while hiding it
    at the same time with his fingers —

and the sly grin, cutting into the right sag
of his mouth as he slowly takes
    a puff of the Marlboro cigarette —

and then lets the smoke curl up into the pupils of his eyes
and then up past the blotched wash of his scalp

where it then wanders over his head like a satin curtain —
    as if it's a vapor trail of some secret inside him

air-brushing through the gloom of day to the window pane
    where it flotillas there, a soft
    amalgamation of soot and dust

mingling there with a hypnotized house fly
trying one last time to blaze through the window —

while outside in the hallway
an orderly brings a deck of cards to us.

2.

Mornings, the sparrows shot like razors
    down across the pavement

that was forever cracked and on those mornings you'd take her
hand as you walked her to the high school,

so full of hesitation in your heart because
you wanted so bad to confess to her

that you knew all about her sister's drugs

and her stepfather's creepy utterings –

and the soft red cut across her wrists that resembled
the edge of leaf lettuce

but instead you stepped in front of her,

lifted the match to the dangling cigarette in her lips,
and you lit it for her…

her lips, the color of leeks when you bent close
to kiss them warm in the January wind
of that terribly cold winter,
the ruts in the middle of the road, stiff and frozen.

3.

The tips of the flame resemble pitcher plants consuming the stars
is what the girl from Nova Scotia said to the newspaper reporter

covering the midnight demolition fire
that consumed the night sky over the old Studebaker Plant

as it burned like a feudal castle to the ground
along Piquette Avenue …

It blazed to ashes. All our monuments blaze to ashes.

Everything you love *a sun*, blazing to vapor and ash.

And the Japanese film crews fell to their knees
to film the hot flames and the smoke's lustrous obscenity.

It was as if the burning buildings – across the glaze of the city
during the Devil's Night fires – were also sacrificial altars.
The street lights so clogged with smoke, like smoldering roses.

4.

When you played cards the old man would quietly sip
his liquor, smoke, and curse the Soviets that took Prague,

and he'd crush the ice in his fingers.

5.

So when she rolled over to her stomach on the bed,
        her young back, tanned, except for the bare shoulder blades

where the swimsuit straps had sautéed her
like the body of a trembling yellow perch,

the warblers outside the window pane descended
like shooting stars over the Rose of Sharon

blooming in her parent's front yard and you saw
where she'd been *burned* – at least it looked like it –

the mark, a birthmark, or a bruise the color of a sugar beet –

one solitary sugar beet shape on her right shoulder blade
        and you softly put your puckered lips there, *kissed it*,

and, when you asked her about it, she blinked at you,
and she didn't say anything at all except for that
she was mesmerized by the sound of a hissing campfire –

(the volatile fire, crackling in a tiramisu mist;
    the sugar beat red-lipped flames;
and her wide eyes the color of verbena
    and star-struck radiance

when you first noticed her at that Oktoberfest bonfire
the autumn you two first met –)

and she looked right into your face for something
you could never really give to her,

and a dog, barking at the next door neighbor's house,

barked, it seemed, until the clouds balled up

into dissolving, rum-stained smoke –

6.

and it seemed only a few months later
she was involved with that older boy

who hiked up into the rhododendron gardens
and he put a gun into his mouth

like he was a large mouth bass turning his face
through water moss to the rising sugar moon

in a kind of obsessive, aquamarine rapture,
and, in the horrible moments that followed thereafter,

the holy smoke
rose over the valley where other campers had lit

a slew of hissing campfires — I was one of them

shoving log after log into the tangerine flame —

and the moon evaporated like a nicoise olive —

and it became a large mouth bass rising up out of pond scum

through a *crème de rose* of clouds.

7.

For years, the vacant grounds sat haunted like a cemetery
fatted with Norway rats and rock pigeons

after the Studebaker Plant burned. You smoked there alone.
Read through the pages of Exile and the Kingdom.

Once, inexplicably, you saw a rose blooming there.
Another time you saw a pheasant unlock the playing cards
of its bright tail wings.

8.

And after the old man expired, the orderlies
rolled the sheets off his bed

where just hours earlier
he'd died on his back, his arms spread like some rotted plant
finally done with it,

the old man from Prague —
who worked at Fisher Body Plant —

and the one gentle orderly — a black woman
who sometimes sat still with him and

read his Bible to him
and smoked with him

and secretly passed the bottle of liquor to him

as the vespers softened the hard night

and the radio station nearby played

classical music until he slept –

she told me, when pulling me close to her,
that he'd asked for *me* –
if I was coming back to play cards with him

that day – it was a Friday in the late summer –
because he had something to give to me:

and, you know, it was the bottle of liquor he'd
        hidden from me inside the gut of his chair.

The liquor resembled smoke curled up
like sphagnum moss in a bottle

and it was half-rotted, half-stoned;

and he'd also left – for me – a letter his wife
        had written to *him*, years earlier;

he'd wanted me to have it:
        she'd written it *to* him:-
a love letter about the smoke

rising rust-like over Prague that spring
when the military troops came

and took the both of them away –
    separated them really in the end –

but you know, dearest heart,
that the smoke
    had somehow turned our gray eyelids
into custodians concealing our true names,
    so desperate not to be revealed —
our hearts' like red roses, corked in glass…

"we're just stretched skin over rose vapor,"
    she wrote to him —
"the least and the most of us
    set into flame

where we tweedle and we flare
while in love, while expiring …"

9.

Later — after he died — after I pushed through the glass
door of the nursing home to my parked car

and I pressed my car key into the ignition,
I heard the loud summertime crickets beneath the rose bush
chirruping wildly

like parsley root exploding,

and they chirruped like hundreds of fireworks
    igniting —

igniting and vaporizing the tangled roots and wounds
of everything in the area surrounding me:

all the blessed babies and the elegant apartment buildings
lighting to fire over Prague, over Detroit,

over the tormented high school girl with the yellow perch
wiggling down over her bare shoulder and across

her beet red bruise
and deep inside her alert, ignited eyes;

and the fireworks ignited in the braid of olive-stained smoke
        rising like a school
of large mouth bass on fire from the cracked-open roof
of an arsoned apartment building that had just exploded
and had collapsed into the shimmering conflagration
        of the torn-apart city; and we could see

all the buildings — like marvelous orange dahlias — blooming
        in flames
as their walls buckled down in a torpor over the sidewalk's refuse
of bricks and its catastrophic soot and ash;

and I remembered that, while walking through the pungent pine
woods one evening in Southwest Florida,

years later — all by myself long after I'd fled Detroit's sadness —

that I found
a small glass pendant lying still in the dead palmetto leaves:

it was fogged-up in a moist mausoleum of pond backwash:
just a small ovular locket — its glass face smoked and splotched

and glazed over
by old dreams, by sago pond weed, and by bur marigold heads —

and I swear to you, dear reader, dear one who follows
        love's smoke,
that someone's private memento —

someone's heart-shaped rose petal — hidden in a lover's locket
        like a promise and rebirth for our future —
was revealed to me (*a precious souvenir*) right there, inside it.

Desultory Refrain for Packard Plant, Detroit

Except for the forgettable,
splintered mounds of snow
bulldozed here – crunched down
like coal-stained peridot
with the blackened grit of winter's
dirt and salt defacing them –
all that's left here now is a hollow building
collecting what happens
to the nameless.
The men who deserted
this factory of Packard automobiles
must have scorned the celebratory
sound of Being –
how its voice, like a fingerling
of trill notes
must have seemed too popular
and too positive,
too dense with families gathering
for small, intimate picnics
on the river where the water
lurched, then plunged into green iron
as the tankers pushed their heavy,
dinosaur bodies forward,
toward St. Lawrence.
And the gulls – lively chanteuses
of manic laughter –
rose above the tidal river bank
in a kind of ceremony
only a blissful eroticism remembers.
History, like memory, *is* porous.
Things fall through it as easy as salt.
Once, before I too was robbed
at gun point, by someone young enough
to be the boy who rakes my leaves,
I believed Time had a desultory
whisper to it –

and that, like the gentle touch
of a woman on a picnic with me,
Time, too, would
wander from subject to subject,
eager to unravel, like a loose scarf,
the indescribable
incommunicable intimacy
of itself,
and, afterwards, when the boy ran off
with all my money,
I too understood the heavy desire
of pornography,
and that it, too, would be born in time.
And so the profiteers, those hiding figures
with gold time pieces and handkerchiefs
in their extraordinary suit coat pockets,
left town, like all the rest of us —
the ones who made this place ours —
and they drove away in lacerating
stretch limousines with rear fenders
cut in the shape of a shark's fins
to attend their board meetings,
or their property summits,
or their conferences regarding
subsidy allowances
and charity endowments for women
whose well-crafted cheeks
were smooth, clear celestine.
And the clean rooms here —
those offices where men did their business
with one another
and where the dust particles today,
right now even, fall as lightly
as brittle stone fairies
shattering and disintegrating
in the de-industrialized half-light's
hypnotic medium
and where Time is a divesting body
not really even able to love itself

as it weaves inexorably
into its apocalypse refrain – even
these rooms are just necklaces of dust.
Ten years ago, I *was* in here –
walking the paths of disintegration –
my stomach, empty,
only to discover that I wasn't
really hungry for Time after all
but finally and only
for the fully abandoned,
absolute utter erasing
of oblivion's clean, clear light.

Cass Corridor Epistle

I remember sitting on the front steps
of the Verona apartments where Joni Mitchell,

hiding up there behind her turret windows,
wrote *Both Sides Now* on an acoustic guitar

while below her, the college students in their
black glasses and their shaggy hair walked

arm in arm past one another to their classes
at Wayne State University. Days far past all that,

when *I* lived in the Corridor, long after Joni
had left Detroit and she'd moved to Los Angeles,

this would have been in the days of 1981 or so –
in the after-burn of Detroit's insurrection

and after the bold hammers broke the buildings
to pieces and nothing but the back doors

of residences remained secretive and friendly
and where people passed gifts to one another –

we'd gather at Alvin's bar to listen to punk
music blast open a Friday evening's silence.

We'd pay, just to see local bands cut noise there.
We'd hang around the tables, drinking beers.

Other bands – *Shadowfax, Bill Hodgson & Friends,
The Rockabilly Cats, Detroit Blues Band* –

jammed there as we kids all clung to each other
mid-dance, holding history's fragmented pieces

tightly to our hearts, because we too, were
splintered, fractured, just keeping time together,

and the air, stalled over I-94, resembled grapes.
History's a slipstream of living water.

Like a stream it carries multiplicities.
Nothing's simple, in history's stream.

"I remember," is how history speaks to us…
It says, "memory's an intentional shaft of light

opening a crack into this fallen world we knew…
Love's the drum stick on which we pulse."

Across taut guitar strings all this wild creation
and lyricism jams on, strummed into tunes, or

into hymns to be sung for a consecration of life.
This corridor's two scriptures: *now and then.*

Once I watched a man blowing his saxophone
above I-94. He was facing south, downtown.

Was he playing to the glory of a necessity –
between the now and the then of everything?

His saxophone transformed my heart's anguish.
Memory's an impassioned madness. It's an

interior monologue that penetrates all loss.
It binds every souvenir the body loses, to time.

Once, walking past Alvin's bar, when I was
in a continuous revelation, history's spirit

spoke directly to me from love's distant body,
and it said to me, "accept" all loss forever…

Forever's that special time clock you'd enjoy,
placed on your side table, for company.

Time's the hand grenade you love that's always
exploding what we love to pieces. It's utterly

faultless, time, because it refuses keepsake to
anything claimed. It's a friend without fidelity.

Once – yesterday in fact – I stood here
where Alvin's bar was; and *time*, so ineffable,

chimed on. It chimed for me, for you,
for all of us singing to the evanescent, again.

Letter to Jack Ridl, from Marshall's Bar

Jack: just a short postcard. I'm drinking
at Marshall's dive bar, on East Jefferson,
just outside the Harbor & Klenk canal
communities in the D. The bar's dark,
and it reminds me of an LA bar I was at
once, where I saw Kiefer Sutherland.
The canals back here remind me of
Amsterdam or Venice, because they're
intimate, and so improbable in the D…
I saw a small shanty boat floating through
here with friendly, overly intoxicated
people on it. The boat resembled an
old grocery store, floating on wood.
The people were jovial as they waved
at me, looking like they'd crawled up
from some embankment of wet mud.
Jack, I'm worried the working class
are all sinking around me in their boats.
Sometimes, silenced by progress or
theft, whole epochs of people vanish.
We exist, whether we're affirmed
or denied. That's my main message here.
Even those *denied* still hold a place here.
At Marshall's bar they offer a tour
of the canals, called '*Boats, Booze & History*,'
because legend has it folks ran booze
through here during prohibition. Next
door is Moe's Bait shop, where they
sell red worms, wax worms, crawfish,
green worms and leeches, night crawlers.
It sounds like characters out of a good
Stephen King novel. Jack: more and
more I'm agreeing with Jean Genet
when he said, in The Thief's Journal,
"we are fallen during the time we bear
the marks of the fall." Now, isn't that

the true circumstance of what it is to
be the injured, the shunned, cut off
from the rest of society? Jack, whatever
happens here, in the D and the world,
don't forget that you and I wrote to
uplift the aggrieved and the broken,
and in so doing, we consecrated them.

Kevin's "Four Roses for Debi"

— On the secretly blushing cheek is reflected the glow of the heart
                Soren Kierkegaard

My twin brother Kevin is at his easel,
            painting four roses for Debi.
                        He's decided to title the work:
                                    "quatre premier amours pour Debi."

This is at 457 East Kirby, and the injured winter skies
            above us — over Detroit,
                        over its cataclysmic ruin —
                                    resemble juniper berry

(there's just enough sharp blue tones up there
            to convince me). He's not quite satisfied
                        with the surface
                                    and so he pivots, stands back,

grips at his chin, sips a beer, steps back, strides
            forward, grabs a razor blade
                        and he cuts the entire surface
                                    to bits.

It would be a gross error to assume
            that this first causal action determines
                        his intent. No.
                                    He's inside the slipstream.

He's inside the chaos. He no longer goes
            from any one fixed point to another:
                        instead, he begins from *any* point
                                    and he proceeds.

Stunned at this, I sweep backwards, stare at him.
            He's acting out the pronounced
                        gestures of love itself:
                                    frenetic, rash, lawless.

157

He oscillates back and forth,
        slicing the painting's surface;
                and then he moves in closer to it,
                        intimately brushing

the flakes of paint off it. They fall to the floor,
        and sometimes he collects them
                in a small mayonnaise jar;
                        and he shakes them all together

and then he reapplies paint to canvas. I stand back,
        observing how he torments
                the whole surface
                        of the painting

by adding an oddball ornamentation to it.
        He stamps hard pennies on it;
                he indents the canvas. He defaces it.
                        He lacerates it with a knife

and then he cuts idiosyncratic squares into it.
        There's a clear technique here:
                he's disfiguring the painting's surface,
                        and he's peeling away

time itself. Now he drives the edge of the razor blade
        cross-cut over the entire canvas
                until he achieves just
                        enough disturbance there

to alarm. Then, in quick succession,
        he sketches the four roses:
                three along a horizontal line,
                        placed juxtaposed,

and a fourth one – *the one exceptional rose* –
        hanging there
                like a suspended inamorata
                        strung up in eternity

just below the other three. To secure the rose,
            he renders a diagonal line,
                        and he traces it into the painting
                                    from the left

down to where the one solitary rose,
            just like a pinned, pendulous corazon
                        fleshed in pinkish melon
                                    and collared in a satiny white,

floats there – isolated – pulsating like a living heart
            throbbing with the breath of life
                        and thump-kicking itself right back
                                    into universal bloom.

I think he's at the collective assemblage of all
            true proclamation: the one rose –
                        as a boundless act
                                    of countenance:

the one single rose acting *of* itself, from its own signal…
            the other three roses strung together –
                        like a bouquet of bridesmaids…
                                    And the one singular rose:

hanging, swaying, *extenuated* –
            the one alive rose, risking itself at edge of love.
                        Yep, he's on it:
                                    love's born in a singularity first;

it's so unique; it's so distinctive: the one rose, floating there
            below the other three roses.
                        Besides – solitary, insulated, immune –
                                    don't we all thrum awake?

Yes: if all singular essence thrums itself awake
            we arrive at a faith
                        in the distinction of all testimony…
                                    To respect the holy day

159

of the one individualized rose.
> Its singular pronouncement.
>> Yes: the pronouncement of the one true heart,
>>> dangling itself out for love.

Or this: the one suspended, exalted rose –
> as the rallying cry of how we
>> hurl ourselves
>>> into eternity's boundless arms.

The one solitary rose –
> as the spirit's incomparably thrown heartbeat.
>> So: it's *heartbeat* he's after.
>>> The one heart, beating in the temporal,

and then lifting itself up into the universal…Everything, all else,
> follows the one singular rose
>> into the universal bouquet of the infinite.
>>> *This one rose as the heart-full-of-soul.*

The one painted rose – bearing the heart's homecoming
> right across the secretly blushing cheek
>> of the canvass's multi-textured face:
>>> *quatre premier amours pour Debi.*

And then – after he's gazed out
> the bay windows at a winter sky
>> that's clouding over the city's sharper edge –
>>> he adds a conflicted flourish

of storm clouds
> across the rose painting's canvas,
>> and he saturates it
>>> with splices of ghosted azure blue;

and he adds in smudges and irksome blots
> of pickle green to create
>> the roses' stems.

Across the painting's

cosmetic face he adds
        an exasperated coinage
                of stamped, vagrant,
                        and deliberately

indented circles —
        small mandalas
                meant to capture
                        and to confuse

the viewer's eye
        and to intensify the indescribable
                in the entire character
                        of the finish

(the indescribable being just
        the openings, *the cracks*, the fissures
                upon the surface
                        of the knowable world

that rifts open the gates where we seek
        one another within the true infinite…
                and not just within time's
                        measured temporalities –)

and, nomadic itinerant squares,
        curls, x's and o's,
                smothered there
                        in the painting's

disrupted textural surface glare;
        and, then, scraping more paint
                off it as if he's obliterating
                        the grotesquely temporal —

that fixed time within the identity
        of the art piece — he finds it,

the one rose's infinite heart:
               look at it: it's floating triumphantly

there for Debi, for all of us —
          it's solitary, it's serene, it's so singular —
               eternalized by light, by time,
                         by infinity, forevermore.

Letter to Terry Blackhawk, from Mt. Hazel Cemetery

Terry: I'm writing you from Old Redford,
in the neighborhood where I grew up in.
I'm wanting to confess to you how I turned
myself from someone I knew, into a writer.
The house I was born in, on Clarita, blew up.
Some report it was a drug deal gone sour.
I remember – with my twin brother – playing
hide and seek at Mt. Hazel Cemetery there.
How we'd hop behind the small sad graves
and then we'd hurl sticks at one another. How
we'd scale the sloped hill and bury ourselves
in the tangled weeds and the leaves. We'd hide
from what we'd learn years later was our
identity, our self-representation. Something
in it, that viscid self-construct, would unsettle us.
So we'd undress our names by becoming others.
So young, we'd become Daniel Boone, Mingo.
Or Batman, Robin. We'd transmigrate identities.
One following the other into a great heroism.
One chasing the other into pure non-substance.
To act, you know, in one's name, takes a lifetime.
It's an act of devotion, stepping into an identity.
And yet, to escape the name is to escape all effigy.
To flee the name's to court enflamed abandon.
Terry, Detroit fell apart. Some vast furnace flame
wrote it into a dead letter and then burned it…
The city packed up its suitcase, it went down
the road. Son House said, "*I'm gonna get me religion.*"
He said: "*you know I wish I had a heaven of my own.*"
Years later, slightly intoxicated by the manner
in which the city's rosary of colors tormented
the tilt of the parkside hill as the sun set –
turned the whole slope into a florid likeness
of bougainvillea as the sundown crawled into
every shadow of the park until the hillside cried

163

itself out with a resurrected beauty – I chose
my seat, right here by Son House's grave, just
off Lahser Road, at the Mt. Hazel Cemetery.
I yelled out his song, Preachin' the Blues. One
sister cried out from behind a small apple tree,
"why don't you just hush?" Another sister –
dressed in many-tongued rags – called out,
"you know he's abandoned, hush your fuss."

Sea Gull, on the Delray Bridge

Now,
>   an afternoon sunset
>>   the murky hue of drought beer
>>>   begins its polluted descent

across the Delray Bridge —
>   here, in southwest Detroit —
>>   where the black piles of slag
>>>   host exalted white sea gulls

and swooping marshmallow clouds,
>   and the tired stroll of working men
>>   to the dive bars, begins again.
>>>   Now the cornstarch sunset

shingles across the bridge,
>   and the lazy, tethered boats
>>   bobbing sideways
>>>   in the golden oil-green broth

of the Rouge River,
>   are momentarily stirred
>>   in the breeze's onset,
>>>   and they linger there,

caught like slabs of salt pork
>   until a slough of clouds
>>   obscures them,
>>>   and the sunlight shingles

across the backs of boys
>   riding their bicycles home
>>   over the bridge's terminus…
>>>   and a solitary sea gull

lands quickly on a piling here,
        and he squawks mightily –
                as if a pebble were caught
                      in his throat –

and he shouts out loud
        in a kind of hunger or protest,
                like a dissident coughing out
                      sound and fury

to the end of the day,
        to the close of summer, to the end of time here.
                Yesterday I stood here,
                      feeling the sturdy bridge

with my hands again,
        gripping it tightly.
                I've come back to it,
                      readying myself again

for god knows what –
        for the ending days of summer
                that will burn away
                      all the light and warmth

within me to the harsh winter winds again,
        to that sudden chill in the air
                tasting like salt-rising bread –
                      my face, turned into it,

and exhaust stench,
        dousing my lungs with delivery truck soot.
                We are young once,
                      our throats clogged

with pebbles and passions,
        with the poetics of the eternal within us
                as we ride our bicycles,
                      or stroll from the bars, back home.

Let me remember this sea gull —
    strident here —
        shouting out loud
           his sound and his fury

into the heap of this voiceless black slag.
    He's shrieking his name —
        the poetics of his vast might —
           into bold vibrancy.

Letter to J. Alfier, from the Rouge River, at Delray

1

Once you were holed up in an uncelebrated city.
Lost among lonesome buildings and soiled fields.

Cars and bars and too much afterthought,
and a grief that fell over you like winsome fog

after you had done wrong, and you knew it,
and you didn't even know why you knew it,

except for the way your hands shook like clams
when you hung the telephone up, after whispering

a broken apology – before the other could even
answer the telephone call in her pajamas.

And later, at another jukebox, you whispered
that you were a foolish man with an injured idea.

2

Sadness is a wormed fruit on a tree that you reach for.
It's a glass of hot beer at three in the afternoon.

It is one of the apples in the original garden, and
the bartender wears a waxy smile. Serves it up.

In the back seat of a taxicab you asked to be let out.
And you found a vacant lot to unmask yourself.

You roamed back in there, through weeds and rubble.
Sea gulls objected to your presence. So did a feral cat.

So did all your sadness. It pushed you into a grave.
All your senses filled with it, like an hypnotic flower –

168

something alive and aromatic, and busy with bees
and tiny arrangements. Startled voices.

You kept up the walk until you reached a fence.
Down through it you crawled, into dark brush.

3

Only when the sadness lifted did you find it:
this clump of swamp buttercup beneath the bridge.

And happy birds, singing in an alcove where
branches cathedraled over an unsung trail that fell –

like sorrow's daughter – down to a friendless river.
And standing there, where ducks sliced open

the oily ribbon of water and lilies emerged
like white and yellow benefactors on a quiet scroll

meant for only those willing to unravel it,
you watched the sunlight parading and grooving

over solitary waves caught up in an insipid laughter.
All our sadness lives inside a tormented wind.

Nothing in the mind knows how to combat
a private, tormented wind. Only stillness moves it.

A small frog leaped into a carnival of bugs.
Broke them apart, like a gossip's conversation.

4

Up in the bur-reeds, a restless wind fiddled a violin
across the stands of browned cattail tops,

and the ripe and clumsy intrepid nutlets bongoed on.
A happy woodpecker hacked away at a tree.

Down the Detroit River, a tanker sledged forward
in a mordant quietude that felt like it was dying.

Your heart – like shunned light, a beautiful power –
burst open, and it spilled all over your boots.

At the shore, you fell to knees, drunk on the world.
Let go what must go, be gone, be something greater.

Letter to Jeff Vande Zande from Abick's Bar

– "the water was all around him; he felt his own strong fins,"
Into the Desperate Country

JV: I'm writing to you from Abick's Bar,
on Gilbert Street in Detroit.
The joint's one of those great old time
neighborhood dive bars you'd find
still active in Chicago. Maybe on some corner
in Saginaw. The guy next to me's telling me
his divorce will cost him about
the same price as getting his appendix
removed. You must be asking, how the hell
much is that? He calculates at least $35,000 –
no worries, since he's just got canned
from his job. A plumber. The woman customer
complained he'd been too *familiar* with her,
called his boss and, as they say, the rest is
"time's-up" history. Didn't we used to worry
our poems would be fair and just and true?
There's no such thing as guaranteed fair play.
This guy tells me he'd rather lose his damn
appendix than give her and her attorney
the satisfaction of robbing him blind.
Says he might traffic in laced weed if it
gets too hard. That is, unless weed's legalized.
Then he tells me he might move into a trailer
with his brother-in-law in Texas. Sell guns.
Time beats us up until we're lame, he says.
Is that the Relative or the Absolute?
Is that the Midwest motto? Detroit's? Maybe his?
Mostly, you take your chances with real estate
and love here. Either way, you repair what's
worthy and salvageable, or you bail out
on what gets lost in the movement of hurt.
And that's toughness, Detroit style. Love it
or leave it: the absolute in the relative.
That's what always *struck* me about Detroit:
Something here got so damn lost in the hurt,
and it might not ever come back. We have

171

to be careful about at which moral level
we *place* the Relative alongside the Absolute.
Isn't that what morality is? How we recognize
the Relative within the Infinite? Either way,
I figure betrayal's always at the scene of these
dramatic fidelity-based crimes. Infidelity, deceit,
glad-handing – these are the characters in
every crime. Detroit's ass was kicked by
these kinds of crime. Some guys accept
and deal in bad cards and they grind on.
In a world of broken plumbing, I think
we've done well, my friend. We've made a
poetics of our lives. I figure everything's
alive in the name we give it. Isn't that placing
the Relative, right here inside the Absolute?
You can't love the Other, the friend, the place, the spouse,
and be Indifferent. No way. There's perpetual
Christmas lights – white bulbs – here at Abick's.
They light up the darkness. You *can* love an
emptiness till it loves you back. I figure that's
faith-based-love. It's Detroit's best hope... JV:
remember that night when we had too much
wine and then we started up the foolish road
of discussing "the writer's life?" You worried
that my writing about the D so much would
confine me to being "just a writer of place."
That book I wrote, *Beautiful Rust?* We toured it,
you and I, up through Saginaw, Bay City,
West Branch, and then you and Josh drove
down here to see me, and you read with me
at that now closed Art Gallery on Michigan
Avenue: remember that homeless shelter
across the way from it? The sign on the side
of its building that said: "Believe *On* the Lord
Jesus Christ and Ye shall be Saved."
Faith in *absence* – always a perilous bet. Try it!
Or those phone calls together where we
cried together over how love gets stripped
away by vagrant stars and white blossoming

172

trees in other men's yards? We can be perfectly
pure and yet as bitter as acrid fruit. You knew it
and you did everything in your power to
never doubt your veneration for life. God I
loved you for your refusal to give it all up.
For you, love's physical: it edifies or forget it.
You just won't deceive yourself for the
sake of the individual self. You don't trust
the self, and that's what makes you moral.
Long ago, you learned that the self's a deer,
it runs frenetic. It's best to aim right at it,
steer into it like a skid, get out of its way.
You'd tower over me, a lazy cigarette in your
hand, and pull me close to you for the hug
hello again. If faith supposes anything's
possible, you pushed the sky higher above
you; you strengthened yourself against its weight.
In *Into the Desperate Country* – your book – you
wrote how in the in between, we give away
what divides us against ourselves or others.
Are bodies are made of rivers. We flow on.
The great danger – of course – was that we'd
fall in love with the D or the self, like they
were real things. Gift them with a grand poetics
of romance and grace. Be seduced by the D,
the self, until they beat us lame...JV: we could
never trust either. You can't trust in a place
or an self that expresses ideas that defile it still later...
But we can love *hope*, like we'd love an absent
God. *Yes*. The guy at the bar, $35 K poorer,
asks me, *yo, do you believe in the D's transcendence?*
Gee, what's the mathematics of transcendence
in the D but 8 Mile Road, the outer
boundary of Detroit? It's a thick *self*. It's muscled by
by electrical power lines, factories, strip joints,
resale shops, salvage lots, tool and dye joints,
used car lots, hair salons, bars...JV: I once
knew a stripper there who danced one of the
seedier Go Go bars to closing. She was –

173

by my best impression – petite, brunette,
and plenty nasty in the morning without
a smoke; she was a coke chick, fatherless.
She had a poodle. Wore curlers for her
morning phone-sex job. *You can see the halo
of transcendence from 8 mile*. It's timid at first,
aping Detroit: Beat up houses, junkers,
foreclosure problems, Medicaid. But further
to the north – where the sea of new buildings
stretches straight up, indicating new wealth –
you can drive into gated coteries, gilded
estates, and seven-figure condos where
Jaguars, BMWs, sit. And women wash
their faces in the morning not to fly ash
or to men fist-fighting over sex or dope,
but to clean clear basins made of marble,
light. Even still, here at Abick's where I'm
enjoying a drink and writing this letter
to you, *life*, you know, dear friend, what we
made of it, from this *deep faith*, is just great.

Letter to Tobi Alfier, from Heidelberg St.

It's mostly color here, I must tell you:
colors of astonishment and glee, both,

this drawing, here on a well-trod road
outside a broken home, in Detroit.

The chalk drawing's been made
to introduce a puppet theater:

a theater, mind you, made of
a brown washing machine box,

and another, smaller side table box,
flushed with a vase of sunflowers.

The box theater's been abandoned:
its inner troupe of stuffed animals

and brown paper bag puppets,
left to dwell alone in silent rehearsal.

And, on the grass, a little girl's
box of crayons and her chalk —

I can tell, because she's left her
Barbie dolls and her pink shoes behind.

I must tell you, I'm a fool for beauty:
every part of me submits to it.

But look here at what's been drawn:
a tall, exited declaration of chalk angels

drawn to human size on the sidewalk
have thrown me into this tizzy.

The angels form a posse of soldiers,
navigating the way to the theater.

Here's one to talk about: a male:
the spectacular halo, drawn in pink,

the wings, like blue feathers of fog,
blurred beyond the star-struck body.

I must tell you, I clamor for beauty,
but I couldn't have expected this:

the angel's neck is strung with lime green
pearls, and black ravens heralding

God above. I must tell you, the one
who drew this angel must be

blind, because she's seen the sound
that eyes, gazing up to Heaven, make,

when they are colored indigo.
I must tell you, this little artist

must be made of holy water
and golden hosannas, her skin

the tint of tomorrow and thereafter,
her small hands, like birds, flying away.

I must tell you, this chalk drawing's
turned me into a pilgrim:

I'm on my hands and knees,
my nose up close to it, praising it.

The Night My Brother & I Were Bats

We're a group of bones made of afterthoughts,
my twin brother and I,

two men out on the town like fruit fly bats,
our small blinking eyes, fervid, alive,

the colors of desire, being: roast pepper,
lady Baltimore cake, strawberry meringue

and Nina Simone bending over a microphone
boiling the song into a chilaca chile –

her voice breaking the song's words apart
with smoky lust and a sizzling anger –

while we danced

to the moon rising over the David Stott building
in Detroit,

while we walked under it, noticing the lights.

~

Someone in a back alley, lighting a joint,
three women in pumps, hustling away

to a waiting Uber cab, the one of them
dropping her pump behind her, losing it

down along Library Street
outside of Vincente's,

then bending back over herself to retrieve it,
slip it back on over her roaming heel

~

while you watched, then later noticed

how a man's small bat nose tastes perfume

when it approaches the mescal,
blue agave, smoked-pepper aroma

of a woman dancing exalted and alone
on a dance floor like a restless

sapodilla tree, lost in a Caribbean wind
among a group of others – young hipster boys
in big glasses, slim kids in tight jeans
and embroidered hoodies,

and dancing women hurtling their hair
down over their pale faces and shoulders
in a charcoal-roasted starlight;

their miniskirts and mojito mouths
checkered by the pulsing polka-dot of lights;

and the music, throbbing through spirals
of amber yellow and grenadine red –

while her mouth, awash in a mulled wine,

tasted of cinnamon, cloves, allspice
as you danced together, pulled each other tightly
to each others' ribs

at a club where the DJ played 45s –
King Coleman, Edwin Starr, Hector Rivera –

~

and her young hips rose up
to your hands and she wiggled

into a tangle of bones made mostly
of afterthought and reverie –

the color of stardust being a mixture

of Ceylon tea and amethyst sugar,
something you can't ever really grab –

while the pungent smell of marijuana,
wafting over the heads of dancers,

spun us into hallucination and laughter

until we left there,
walked back home under a chestnut

roasted moon rising over
the David Stott building in Detroit –

and we followed it, the merry moon,

as it skipped away from us,

down along the cobblestone streets
of Corktown – that night, long ago,

when my brother and I were bats.

Letter to John Jeffire, from the I-75 Bridge

J: I'm writing to you from the I-75 bridge,
where below me, the Rouge complex is on fire.
The flames, bursting and flaring out of stacks,
resemble the finger tips of Lucifer, getting
some sort of manicure here. The whole sky's
olive-green and sleekly nauseous. And the smell:
it vaguely carries the stench of sulfur – like
a seething decay – just like the way a user
smells, coming off a bad narcotics bender. Wicked.
That whole inner organ – combusting thing.
Hell, you know it: fire, becoming a death furnace.
Addiction, ambition, all the same neuronal hit.
We sure confuse aggression with passion.
Birth and blossoming… becoming confused
with fiery conflagration. Maybe that's how
all our bad habits start. God, I loved your novel,
Motown Burning. Here's the ontology of it:
either love your big wounds enough to accept
them, or you'll never heal them. I figure
that you figured out, long ago, that our resilience
is best discovered, found out, or developed
inside an honest wrestling match. So true that.
Detroit, when we grew up there, was indeed
a wrestling match. John, you must have took it
to the mat, working out so many big riddles
inside the clutch, the hold, the slip, the flip.
Detroit cut its big smile off to spite its face.
It's destruction – in a style of purified terror
without a barrier – was too tough for any love
to break down. I figure when the city burned up –
trying to believe in profit while ignoring all
the terror – something inside us all was torched.
Hey, you can't create peace when terror's
the last loud guy staring you down at the bar.
So terror – the flames up 12th & Clairmont –
settled something down in all of us for a bit.

180

One more thing about your ontology: you
believe value passes into the minds of others.
I can see it when you carry that grin, a pride,
into a room with others. It's a pride that
breaks into a kind of wealth. That's good. It lasts.
Everything that lasts will break something bad
that tries to steal it. Maybe that's real change.

To the Broken Statues in a Field, Detroit

There is a place where I could go,
          to die.
                    It is behind a fence,

as all prohibited places are.
          There are a few very fine
                    weather-worn statues

of saints here. The Virgin Mary,
          her blue robes scuffed
                    and lacerated

by the hardness of winter.
          And there is St. Raphael, so lovely,
                    standing inside the scrabble

of a chair – his one wing, shattered,
          and yet – like something forever –
                    he's still grasping

his healing staff.
          The invisible one, who has carefully
                    placed these statues here,

must have dwelled in the rear seat
          of this 1959 Wedgewood Blue Ford Custom 300
                    He would have chewed

on French fries,
          and sent small notes to his friends
                    inside silver-misted vodka bottles –

those vagabond friends
          who've crawled on all fours
                    to hide from the police

in order to pass beneath the chassis' of cars.
       He might have even loved
           a twilight

labyrinth kind of woman
       swathed in a corduroy skirt
           and in a ripped,

onion-colored shawl,
       and on the occasion
           of love's simple design,

he would have held her soft and tender
       as the moonlight split
           her body open,

and the fireflies — hundreds of them —
       surrounded her
           as she, herself,

opened her vast soul to the earth.
       A shattered field is a gate
           of wonder.

The statues there, gathered
       together in solemn pairs —
           some in silent translation —

are speaking in tongues
       all the poems and prayers
           our hearts must hear.

And the small pointless artifacts here,
       so natural and so free
           of any attachment,

confer upon themselves
       a religious rite,
           as if in ceremony.

Is it enough to offer oneself
           to the everything here?
                Is it enough

to have wept away
           all the unwillingness here?
                All this unwillingness

that steels us against
           one another?
                To have found, in one's

swollen eyes, the *other* self —
           The one who will not lie
                when there is suffering.

Is it enough to be honest and to suffer,
           even in this heart-heavy music
                and wind?

What is this but just amorous space —
           right here, in the middle
                of a waste yard?

The statue of Jesus
           with his red ruby heart emblem —
                glowing so solemnly

in March's dull, heartsick gray.
           His arms, open to the flock.
                And the dolorous pigeons,

cooing,
           strengthening their soft cooing
                sounds —

singing this chilled winter blindness
        into a frenzy
                of prophecy.

Is it truly enough to be kind?
        Even when the audible world,
                thick with road rage,

exhausts us so? It's only by
        this elegizing
                that we will capture

how to love a world slowly dying before us —
        one that's still worthwhile.
                Once, squatting here,

I saw how I could perish, you see.
        I saw that when my finger
                accidently

brushed against the statue
        of St. Raphael —
                right over there

on the wounded wing that still
        rose up in a kind of
                fevered festival

so that beyond it one could still witness
        the sad buildings
                of Detroit

holding on like cemented hearts
        still grand and ornate
                in the vaulted archway

of a mustard-stained afternoon —
        that I too, you see, could die
                in this kind of embrace,

without ever second-guessing it.
That I could be *in* this
amorous relationship…

This love sickness – this prayer state –
where my heart is so full
it cannot believe

in anything else –
because to reject any
of these treasures

from myself – this old 59' Ford Custom
and these small statues
in their private gallery –

would starve the very hunger
of my heart
into an empty barrenness.

And so: It is okay to go on,
you little broken angels.
It is okay if people think

I'm a little bit crazy,
because you're continually
speaking in tongues, to me.

Letter to Marcus & Thorburn

Gentleman, I'm writing to you from
23rd Street at Michigan Avenue, here
in the D. I'm a bit north of Corktown.
I've just strolled on foot past the old
Claramunt Printing Co., its insignia still
in prominence against a quiet field of
nothingness. Years ago, after we spoke
together, the three of us, a building
along here – long trashed & abandoned –
had an artist's scrawl moving stealthily
across it that read: "**It Don't Exist.**"
I stepped inside the broken face of the
building & I trampled the wreckage.
All across the inside walls smudged green
was, again, this billboard's declaration –
It Don't Exist. It Don't Exist. It Don't Exist.
Was this some stronger hex, meant to
guard the building from the Voodoo Arts
of a greater vandalism, or was it the more
powerful marquee of a sadder type
of commonwealth – namely – that the
primal form of politics in the D is erasure?
Peter, Russell, I must confess to you
that I'm worried as all hell about just
who controls our future here. *Who?*
Today, rambling through open fields
spread all across the city, I wandered past
old bath tubs & ransacked hulks of cars.
I saw a deserted accordion – soundless –
in a continuous collapse & then I found
someone's mysterious face masks; they
were preserved as heirlooms to some
ancient mysterious rite long ago
completed & then, I guess, forsaken.
And – believe this or don't – down by
the river's seductive olive-stained pallor:

a trinity of dead fish, grouped in place
like arrows pointing directionally at
the city's three corners & a fourth
fish, slanted off to the south, aiming
at the river. Could any symbol, any
God, avert the dangers of dark priests
making their ceremonies against the
light here? Maybe the Nain Rouge
Demon, lurking eerily under the forsaken
washing machines & the dead cast iron ovens
serving as ceremonial altars for those
street priests & those shamans that roam
in and out of the windowless temples
of abandoned homes that safeguard us all here,
is being extinguished like an old flame.
Maybe light & peace are glittering on the
horizon as we hold love inside the chalice
of our hearts for one another & for
opportunities made of the finer crystalline
light of spirit, ascending & descending here.
This truth's being preached at the *2nd*
Chance Ministries on Michigan Avenue
as the thin crucifix, blazing to neon light,
opens up the avenue to jubilant rapture.
Maybe blindness becomes disloyal
to itself, and thus therefore, we see.
Now, down the homesick fringe of
Tillman Street, I see the unconscious
become conscious: he's so finely appareled,
a minor King! His shoulders, draped in fur.
Look: he's feasting on hot chicken wings
& plotting against anything interruptive
across his royal domain. Around him
two, maybe three chairs, & a piano…
some drunken boat of epistle & chantey.
He's pounding a battle march over the
piano keys – against any evil malediction.
Alongside him a minor Queen, waving.

She's robed in fancy lace & a wool scarf.
Her coat's draped with a bridal care-cloth.
Her head, crowned with fake dandelions.
Her cheeks, rouged with charcoal dust.
Now I'm watching them dance their one
Fertility dance of triumph. He embraces
her & she sinks into his robed kingdom –
right there in the *Carpe Diem* of his arms
as the sunset's madness tints them
in a pigment resembling crimson. Now the
wedding ceremony mattress they've laid
upon is suddenly consecrated by a sword
of twilight, washing it in blue smoke.
Every last shred of sunlight evaporates.
Lots candle-flame to softened ash.
Equations of time flatten under shoes.
They stand, facing sunset's royal arms.
I look at them & see History passing
through them like flaming wedding rings.
They sing like Ravens raw as bone.
Now they oil the troubled waters.
They ring the posies for days gone by.
My love & I, until I die. Not two,
but one. Until my life is done. Rave on.
They embrace to protect the candle.
Now they red rose the old Knight.
They waltz for Cupid Stringing his Bow.
Isn't that how Love insists? Always
against Old Mortality, Old News, Old Hands?
Boys, the intelligence to be re-learned here
in this matrimonial field of beautiful rust,
is that Ignorance – the keeper of
the past's terrible simplicity & blindness –
is best conquered by the Seven Spirits
of God seeking scaffolds of light
inside what don't exist what don't exist.
We can only believe when robbed
blind of hope, our seeds, scattered.
Our hands fumbling for our face.

Oh Blessed Soul, beholding how it is
We Don't Exist, We Don't Exist…
We can only believe when we are no one.
Now the King & Queen rise up,
& then the entire Choir of Creation –
all the dusk born birds – begins chanting.
Listen: You can hear it in how they sing
the Shambala divinity of ruby tongues.
You can hear them singing to the change.
Together singing as one. Rave on.

Chinese Lanterns, Cass Avenue

In the chilled autumn Detroit night, a group
of young women have gathered together,

their hands holding these quaint, paper shell
Chinese Lanterns. We walk up to them,

cluster together alongside them, tuck our
necks down into our scarves as the women —

Pagan witches? Sorceresses of conjuration? —
reach lit matches up into the opening

at the bottom end of these floating lanterns,
to set to flame the small candle burners there.

Now, one by one, these rice paper lanterns —
some of them cream white, some red-orange,

some ovular globes adorned with elaborate
Oriental temples or coiled, sprung dragons —

lift up, gently, and they softly ascend over
the cornice tops of the avenue's buildings

and, like weird, glowing prayers, the lanterns
wander and drift like the mind's random

thoughts — into a vast whereabouts unknown.
What does it seem here, to me, but that as I

watch them amassing — like top-heavy moons
up above and over us — that they're prayers

of duration — endurances — for all our old
sufferings and new hopes. They're all rising up —

to extinguish what's now *unfit*. And for what's
been weak, or cruel? what's been noble, grand?

these too, have their own epochs. Even us,
watching them rise, these benevolence lights

enriching us: our hopes made vibrant, again.

Art Installation
— Ryan Doyle's Dragon Gon Krin, "Save the Arts"

The artist had constructed from Midwest metal
a dragon; fire flaming from its gaping mouth,

and a group of evening radicals, tramping around,
had hauled the beast in a truck, unpacked it,

and they'd hoisted it up together in one piece,
in front of the Detroit Institute of Arts.

This was at the first, ice-packed freeze-up *tilt*
of autumn's spirit, where the midnight moon,

glowing like a halo above the slate-tiled roof tops
and the feudal turrets of the old neighborhood,

seemed to furnace-burn the gold and the orange
tree leaves, hanging limp there, waiting to fall.

What makes us dream big? What touched me
as I stood out there in the suspended cold,

gazing at this iron dragon transforming all art
into passion, and the night's darkness, into heat,

the literal back into metaphor, and then back?
The ardor of love's vigor, like a negation of death —

so accessible, so enthralling — where the revival
is suddenly set free in an influx of fiery flames?

Where rebels or just college kids roam free. Some,
arriving here on simple bicycles; some of them

in serene twosomes, embracing one another
in a contagion of intimacy; their arms wrung

around each other's shoulders and their sleeves,
becoming scarves for warmth as the dragon

lit up the night. Monomania of the artist now
becoming all our ardent mania? this rust belt *I am.*

Apocalypse Refrain (Detroit)

In the event of such a sorrowed
ending as the apocalypse –

before we are fomented into the fire's
everlasting heat and its opalescence

because our time here, as mortal beings,
has erupted in a finality and in a blaze –

let me enter into this fanfare a ceremonial
triad of trumpets, all blowing soundly

as the sunset's dandelion haze
tenderly slips behind the row houses

of brownstones and the streets of fire
and along the hungry street corners

that the trumpets mark a lascivious farce
and a lugubrious, if ludicrous fandango

across those folks who've already been blessed
or lost in the decade's delirium dance

of poverty and its crazed mayhem, mixed
with all this uproarious laughter and bold wealth.

All this simply to notice that we have
made ourselves tender with mercy

and also, ferocious with the lobster
red of the sunset's extant blaze.

And let us lift our glasses to the wise,
sprightly up-tempo lift of the piano duet

now being played in an open field
where the red-spotted purple butterfly

and the white admiral lift up and sail –
with several quick flaps and a flat-winged

glide – so amused – over the field
where these two men at the piano take

turns playing a duet to the sunset's opalescent
glare.

Let us calculate the bold lift and glide
of all these innocent butterflies

as they, too, slip and disappear by night's
crepe suzette and its crimson tinting.

Let us notice the mid-drift of the soul
in a butterfly and a bird, chasing

one another over the rounded shoulders
of a statue, here in Grand Circus Park.

Let us notice that we are a simple line
of flight –

inside an assemblage of light. And in
every apocalypse we are a revelation

unveiling upon an open scroll. We're a
new vision upon a dream or its reverse.

All this to make note of the intrepid
pah-pa-rah of trumpets blowing

the evening tide down through the streets
of fire from the open windows,

from the foundations of all our hopes,
and from the unforgettable *doo-wop*

refrain of those shunned
and penniless impoverished folk

standing in groups at the bus stops
their voracious eyes, hungry as birds

who have no less a place here –
as the renaissance of prosperity

emerges for the well-contented,
and the new era's apocalypse begins.

Performing John Lee Hooker's Boogie Chillun

— for Brent Smith & Bryan Lackner

On stage with Passalaqua —
alongside Brent and Bryan —

at the N'Nambi Gallery in the Sugar Hill Arts District
on Forest Avenue, in the D —

performing my poem, *John Lee Hooker's*
Boogie Chillun, Hip-Hop style

and holding faithful to Eddie Logix's mix,
my brother Keith's pulsating bass behind us.

The three of us, dressed in Zoot suits.
The girl singers, trilling behind us.

Does it get any more sizzling
than this? Any closer to a transformative zone?

The three of us as musical Bishops.
The *Boogie Chillun* brought back to life

by three oratory prophets!
Veneration of the worshiped fallen!

Invocation verging on Announcement.
Poetry as dynamic evocation —

deep inside the individual heart
and from the infinite substance.

Down below us the audience surges —
the people sprawl, they elevate —

just like a baptismal levitation in the holy house.
The spirit is generous. It fuels us awake —

this cataclysm of amplified voices —
we feel it awaken the Boogie Chillun, again.

The Starlings over Washington Boulevard

The black-cloaked starlings
      flying in wide schizophrenic circles
           from their roosts

beneath the girders of the Ambassador Bridge, north
      to Midtown, and then,
           rounding up and over

Greektown's low one story buildings
      and then, high over the Eastern Market's
           frenetic commerce,

descend down upon us –
      we who sit here on Washington Boulevard,
           drinks in hand

as the dusk's incandescent care-taker
      rings itself around us
           and softly settles itself

in the friendly linden trees. St Augustine said,
      "love is all fire,"
           and these birds –

ambassadors of love's body
      and carriers of Detroit colossal soul
           that's now rising up

out of its body in a soaring aeroplane
      and gliding out toward its freedom –
           encircle the entire

circumference of the downtown sky
      as they round-a-bout
           through the carbon vapors

of summertime's dusk,
        showing us what occurs
                when pleasure,

for its own sake,
        for want of something better,
                is loved.

Now they lift up again, silhouetting against
        the flat rectangular shapes
                of downtown's buildings.

Are they the city's elation? —
        missionaries from its rigid body —
                flying like free emotion?

Some soar out ahead of the flock
        like pointed arrows nudging ahead
                while others ascend and then

de-escalate behind —
        black striped ribbons
                undulating —

in a to-and-fro parading.
        Now some of the starlings —
                in an apocalypse of landing —

settle thickly into the open branches of the trees,
        their dusk songs, ablaze in sound,
                as if the Universal Self here —

the life force of the city, at once
        fragmented, soaring, flying, splintering —
                could shatter and re-assemble again

amidst these trees planted along the boulevard.
        Maybe love's body — that cluster
                of cells that makes us whole —

is only anointed by its fragmentation, and then, by its
            sudden coming back together again.
                        Maybe these celebratory starlings —

torn aggregates from the Ambassador Bridge's
            lonesome girders —
                        are the lovely limbs

of the city's fragmented self. And maybe they
            return to us — over and over again
                        in this ritual

of impassioned ascent and spiral —
            just to show us all how true fulfillment
                        begins in separation

and then ends in love's unity — as if nothing
            can be whole again until its been
                        torn open first,

and we're turned toward what must be
            renewed again — separation being the gap,
                        joined together, in repair.

Maybe ownership's the culprit here: maybe
            the miracle of incorporation —
                        the self in another self —

is the riddle we're here to break open like a seed:
            Maybe we're here to witness
                        how ownership's

the breakpoint boundary where the spirit of a being
            strangles itself within its conflict
                        of appropriation-into-form

until it becomes what? a winged,
        cold sovereign shadow, suddenly liberated
                and torn free of its source

like these starlings? and, in so doing, becomes
        a fervent cell in love's true body,
                its spirit, so inspired.

Now the three of us, sitting here,
        watch these starlings as they descend
                from the sky into the trees.

Something in us is calmed
        as they land in twos, threes, fours
                into this cluster of trees.

The lovely eyes of the imagination, ours,
        fired on. And dusk — in its intelligent
                grace —

cloaks us in its grand kingdom
        of breakthroughs — with starlings from
                from the bridge to here, and back.

Letter to Joy Gaines-Friedler, from West Village

Dear Joy,
        I've been dwelling in the margins again,
                absorbing the wider distances

between what's a true liberty of merit,
        and what's just a determinable property
                wherein the wealth of things –

these lovely sunflowers growing alongside
        a collapsed front porch –
                begin and end for all of us

living here,
        within the larger incorporated body
        of the D.

Joy, does our ongoing accrual of wealth
        motivate us to become better people?
                Sitting here in this coffee shop,

sipping this exquisite espresso, I focus on
        countless new stories of change
                being told to one another here.

The new vegan restaurants, cocktail bars, the bakeries,
        the sisterhood of yoga studios,
                as if, somehow,

by succeeding we can, what? successfully
        replace it – this embedded generation
                of forsaken displacement –

as if the past and its broken-hearted dreams
        never really happened?
                Let's not fool ourselves here:

no matter where we run
>the wrecked cars, the unoccupied
>>neighborhood roads

fraught with slashed tires, with stray dogs
>and mattress communities,
>>chase right after us all, seeking audience.

The world is always just presentation,
>without *one* possessor:
>>we've been fooled so very long

by this: that the world is best governed
>by one possessor, by one strong overlord,
>>be it by inheritance of the king,

the president, the politburo, the state.

~

Isn't this the great illusion?
>That the future's just another commodity
>>meant to be purchased,

to be seized, appropriated, owned, taxed?
>This testament's so very bound up –
>>and it's hidden and it's concealed

inside our true terror of fair play, diversity,
>difference and of death;
>>we're never *one* possessor....

~

I'm not speaking of Socialism or Communism –
>I'm speaking of the telepathy
>>of the future's *seeds of thought*.

Everything's connected to everything else.
      No hiding it. We inherit every system
          of power leveraged to advantage,

and every system's advantage
      makes new another labyrinth's riddle.
          It shapes who we will be

with one another, unconsciously.
      Is that the myth of the eternal return? Maybe.
          I can't escape it. You know it.

The future's always the telepathy of a distance,
      inching nearer to thee. It's always a fertile zone.
          It incorporates us

into a community space no matter how we deny
      its universality. It depends on everyone –
          all of us – to care-take it forward.

No system of power that negates the future's
      capacity to imagine, and to make real the greater urging
          of us all working together –

(you know the metaphors offered here: lovers, leaders,
      gardeners, worker bees
          map makers, visionaries

collected in a cohesion of dynamic purpose –)
      will provide us lasting peace, fruitful aim, survival…
          The Future's arc is always felt

in the Living tissue of the Collective Being holding Possibility.
      We can't escape how the Collective's Arc
          makes us all feel, or know, or act.

The spectator-future *is* voyeur. This is Freud, Joy –
      writing in his study and warning us
          that we behold: *we are the beholden.*

We always inherit the fair and just result of what
        we've stolen or franchised, prohibited or created,
                or given fairly, without deceit. It just *is*.

The only reason I'm writing this to you, Joy,
        is because I see that the sunflowers here,
                so yellow and so brutal

in their stark un-alterable alien beauty
        and so unregulated as they climb up
                and capture this entire front porch,

resemble – to me – the exact way that the multitude
        of *anything*, when left to design's articulation,
                inevitably becomes the One Power.

The real apocalypse begins
        when fertility and massacre arise
                together, against a world.

In that scenario, the brain stem of anything
        established, explodes...
                The center cannot even hold.

                        ~

So this old east side neighborhood that I'm in
        with all its peculiar symptoms –
                all these ramshackle homes

so decorated with rogue sunflowers
        and snarled green weeds
                climbing up all around them

and surrounding them like green strands
        of greedy fingers
                shading the suspicious, wounded

fully alive faces of its people —
        is just the expressed wish for something new,
           for something irrepressible

and involved, rising towards the very different.
        And this great *dance macabre* —
           all this warfare between brothers

in this place of unresolved disputes, of bar room brawls
        and all these forgotten kisses,
           will become the ancestral dance

of an unrequited *dream* advising us, haunting us…
        We can't escape history.
           Our time's always the future's time.

Who carries the future's time spell forward?
        Who ignores it?
           And the past, like a released convict,

never leaves us…it kidnaps us…
        so we can see *who we've been* with one another
           or who we *can* be.

Isn't this the true call of a greater heroic?
        That we'd all *hear* the call —
           at this stage of history?

And then, do our little part to make a kindness
        an opportunity…?
           And honor the Law of Inheritance

that informs us — right to our face —
        that we're *already* the past, the future,
           living into its image, right *now*?

~

Joy: just today I hiked up the slashed line of Agnes Street
to where Van Dyke
swept boldly toward the river.

I saw, in an old woman's face,
an unbound necessity to be recognized…
by you, by me, by everyone.

She was nudging her grocery cart of garments
down Van Dyke, her ancient eyes
looking right into me

like she could see my gaze aimed to the very
same thing: this intimate,
inspirational embracing

of one another, for the heart's true accrual
of a richer merit.
The divine passed through her,

right into me. That's why I wrote to you, Joy,
in order that I could tell you
the divine —

from this long period of gloom
and sordid repression — is in us.
I walked her to the river's edge,

we hugged, we parted. Behind this action,
I told myself: judge not…
this is just the body,

moving closer toward another body —
shrinking
the distance.

Out of the body the soul arises, a double;
it's always shaped by our consciousness:
we succeed or fail in a total etheric field.

~

Do the others, their wallets fat with cash,
  see it, feel it, the onset of the divine
    here,

inviting us to *shrink the distance*?
    Yesterday, alone and drinking
      at a dive bar

(I won't say which one), a man reflected
    to me that our shared future –
      and how we shape it in *one* field –

becomes our finer apprenticeship
    for an incorruptible unity.
      And together

we grasped the possibility of an ascending
    attention here before not fully felt:
      that love is a commitment duty

that makes rich and fair all true affinity.
    E pluribus unum. Out of the many, the one.
      And from the one, the many.

The man told me he was from Memphis.
    I don't quite recall his Christian name.
      Only that his eyes on mine

as we spoke so gently together,
    as we shaped our conversation's arc
      through its present text

and into its future, made light in me
    a noble consent to always walk upright –
      to stand brave and true –

inside the greater good.

The Monumental Classic Cars go to Heaven

Up Woodward's multi-lane and Gratiot Avenue's
grand emancipation in and out of Wayne County

and, North and South, across Telegraph Road, the
great classic cars push and surge along these paths

en route to Heaven. And like one of the Creator's
directors, I am waving them all in. Look at this one

as it chugs past me: it's a 56' Plymouth; the car's color –
astonishingly – is Briar Rose, its grille, a steel beam

up the center, balanced by a fine metal *insert*, and, above it,
a silver crest with two kneeling warriors hoisting

up bowls of fire. And 55' Chevrolet 210, Glacier Blue,
weaving in and out of traffic, its grille, grinning, and the

amused triangular taillights, buxom red. Behind it,
an asylum fleet of Cadillacs, their rear fins cutting

the air with a sharp mendacity, and a 55' Oldsmobile
swimming behind them and being trailed by a two

57' Ford Fairlanes, one of them Bermuda Blue,
one, Sunset Coral, proving to me that sometimes

there is no death by morbid rust but rather, that
some cars, blessed, ascend on the natural exhaust of air.

And zooming past me now, a 56' Mercury, two-tone:
Glamour Tan, White; its soulful eyes vaulted in arches,

the grille bar, emblazoned with its lettered *nom de plume*,
and, alongside it, a spectacular Green 59' Pontiac,

its ravenous split grille resembling a forest animal,
and a 56' Dodge Coronet, the straight line airfoil fins

opening up into steel chevrons flared with red taillights,
and a chromed a-line freelancing into the bumper.

Now a 59' Buick swerves out lane, its maniacal face
biting the air, its lights triangled by two sharp eye brows

and, behind it, Studebakers, Packards, Lincolns, Ramblers
all roll by us, handmade into the vast suburban sprawl.

Thunderbirds – 1955's and a monster mouth White 58' –
glide past us, tailed by a toothy 54' DeSoto gnawing behind

and, like a globule of Powder Blue, a 54' Kaiser Manhattan
rolls up, halts, dodges past a Spring Mist Green 56' Ford,

and a Bronze 58' Fairlane – its grille, ravenous, sharp-set – chugs
up, pauses, honks twice, and the junkyard angels gather.

A garish 59' Mercury – its enormous red rear taillights lit up
like an Aztec priest – breaks, and a 57' Montclair kicks up past.

Along the road side, we all wave at these cars driving by.
Edsels, Corvettes, and a tail wind of Chrysler 300's – 56's, 58s –

weave in and out of the traffic lanes like metal temples.
The summer air, humid, suddenly mists in awakening.

I pull my wife close to me, hug her as we celebrate the
parading automobiles passing by like transcendent spirits.

Whisper to myself these low prayers to pistons, to grilles;
to bumpers made of scriptures confronting the end of the

world and its drunken madness that we'll all be redeemed
by this myth of fins that delivers us, that consecrates our lives.

Pray too, to be taxied by this majestic parade. In these classic
cars made from devotional will; in these great symbols, of *us*.

A 59' Galaxie, its grille bespattered with stars, drifts by: it's
a Torch Red convertible and the driver, in the front seat,

smiles himself into vapor, and then he fizzles into spirit
just as I wave to him, and then I invite him to ascend in true

apotheosis – full body and soul – into the apogee of all
true luminous appearance; and then he drives right through

the opened gates where Heaven is a classic auto show:
the banner, across the gate, boldly reading, "Welcome

back to Detroit, the Motor City," this second coming,
where all old cars join the gloried kingdoms of the world.

Detroit Doxologies

Praise to Joe Louis's iconic, bold pugilistic fist downtown;
long may we have punch; long may we have reach.

Praise to Hart Plaza's copious water fountain; its throngs;
long may we gather as families; as brethren; as peers.

Praise to the Ambassador Bridge's ample stretch and span
so veiled in mist; long may we greet its reach at dawn.

Praise to the waterfront's hiking paths; the benches; the trails;
long may the ducks and the geese collect there; honk.

Praise to Gratiot Avenue's pawn shops; to Trinosophes. To
the Hardware stores; the eateries; long may we trade goods

for easy cash. Long may we wander into the butcher shops;
shop the street venue spots; kneel at St. Joseph's Church.

Praise to the great new Jazz Café at Music Hall. Long may
we hear trumpets, saxes, drums; torch singers.

Praise to Cobo Arena and its famed rock & roll concerts;
long may the echoes of all those great bands stay.

Praise to the Pistons, the Tigers, the Red Wings and Lions;
long may they handle the movements of game with grace.

Praise to the Dequindre Cut greenway, the walking paths;
the subversive graffiti. Long may the bicyclists peddle there.

Praise to Campus Martius; its ice rink; its fountain: long
may the pigeons and the people meet and greet there.

Praise to Greektown's famous eateries and its Saganaki;
long may we throw dice there. Eat lamb and rice there.

Praise to the Eastern Market's produce; its food stalls;
long may we trade cash for food there. Eat at Bert's.

Praise to the State Fair Grounds and all the animal ghosts
there; long may cattle and cowboys rustle and gallop there.

Praise to Lafayette Park and its young families; its lovers;
long may the dogs run wild after flung Frisbees there.

Praise to the great cemeteries: Mt. Eliot, Woodmere;
Elmwood, Trinity; Mt Olivet; long may we lay there.

Praise to Midtown's sprawl; its university huts; its bars;
long may we recite our poetry there. Our hymns.

Praise to certain iconic bars: The Bronx; Union Street;
The Old Miami; Abicks; Donovan's; Charlie's Bar;

Nancy Whiskey; Temple Bar; Cas Bar; Raven Lounge;
P.J's Lager House; Kiesling; Nemos; The Sugar House; The

Jolly Old Timers; Marshall's; Tom's Tavern; Honest John's;
long may we hoist our glasses there. Why let us toast.

Praise to the Heidelberg Project: its polka dots; its sacred
stuffed animals ascending a house like yearning angels;

its multifaceted faces of God offering each one of us hope;
its animated taxi cabs and its vinyl record hut. And praise

to its creator, Tyree, rambling around his resurrection lots —
a shaman, a warlock — making art from what's been lost.

Praise to neighborhoods: Green Acres; Bagley; Littlefield;
Island View; West Village; Jefferson-Chalmers; Pulaski;

Forest Park; Brush Park; Woodbridge; Delray; East Village;
Rosedale Park; Corktown; Lafayette Park; Springwells;

Belmont; Old Redford; Brightmoor; Briggs; New Center;
long may we salute new babies brought to their life there.

Praise to Motown's echo. To all of Heavy Metal's golden hits.
To Techno Pop and to Hip Hop. To Aretha; Marshall; Iggy;

Jackie Wilson; George Clinton; Barbara Lewis; Smokey;
The Contours; Marcus Belgrave; Mitch; Diana; Thornetta,

Jack and Meg White; Patti; Bob, Berry and the MC5;
long may the air be cut and polished by their songs.

Praise to Hitsville USA, United Sound, the Latin Quarter and
to Baker's Keyboard Lounge, long may they swing.

Praise to our poets: Dudley, Naomi, Ron Allen, Philip Levine;
to Terry, ML, Joy, John, Peter, Jamal; long may you run.

Praise to grand buildings: The Fisher; The Guardian;
The Michigan Central Depot; St. Anne's Church; The DIA;

the Masonic Temple; The GAR; Lee Plaza; The Fox;
Book Tower; The Book Cadillac; Broderick Tower;

The Ren Cen; the Packard Plant and the Fisher Plant #21;
the glass-domed Anna Scripps Whitcomb Conservatory

on Belle Isle; Praise to the grand dame Belle Isle herself –
long may we see our sister city, *Windsor*, glowing there.

And long live the famed brownstones: The Ansonia, The
Altadena, The Cromwell, The Manhattan, The Charles;

and praise to the Forest Arms, The Lawrence, The Milton,
The Knicker Bocker, The Phillips Manor, The Brentwood,

Medbury Place Terrace, The Coronado, The Virello, The Eileen,
The Commodore, The Woodstock and The Barlum Apts.

To Heather Hall, The Renaud, The Elmoore, The Arondo; to
Seldon Manor and The Rinaldo Arms Manor! — long may

they stand strong in the cold. Long may folks huddle upon
their front steps; long may their facades shimmer with sun.

Praise to the sculptures: The Thinker, The Michigan Soldiers
and Sailors Monument, The Spirit of Detroit, Robert Burns,

The Hazen S. Pingree, The Hand of God Memorial (cut for
Frank Murphy): long may they stand guard for who we are.

Praise to the little children — to the boys and girls — chasing
each other through the opened valves of fire hydrants; their

innocent faces reflective of who we are; once were; still can be.
Praise to the cackling, full-hipped women at the laundry mats;

to the working men changing oil in the auto docks; to the boys
shooting hoops on glass-shorn basketball courts. And praise to

the Street God, hidden under his own opposite — upside down —
tearing the mask from his face; praise to him; to his effusive light;

praise to his heart masquerade. Praise to the golden autumn day
he brings. Praise to the goddess statue at the Gas Company,

and the way that she poses to the evening's sun. Praise to
the way that the expansive James Scott Memorial Fountain

on Belle Isle explodes it silvery water way up and then down
onto the generous sprawl of the fountain's basin. Praise to

the feral, orphaned, roaming dogs that consume our refuse;
to the ragged cats that skulk low under broken viaducts;

to the unlawful rats that roam old beams in the emptied hotels.
Praise to the lesser gods and angels – men in furs; women

in head-wrapping dhukus – partying on. Praise to the fine medics
in the ERs that treat us all, that heal us. Praise to the firemen

that quell the devil's powderfinger. Praise to the merciful beat
cops that squat gently to greet the faces of smiling children.

Praise to the reverends, to the pastors, to the tarot healers
who cast their miracles for us; long may they invoke and pray.

And praise to the classic cars: The Chevrolets, the Fords,
the Chryslers, Buicks, Pontiacs and Mercurys and to the Olds

and the Lincolns and the Cadillacs; to the De Sotos, the Edsels,
the Dodges and the rogue Plymouths, the Studebakers

and the Packards, the Hudsons, the Ramblers and Thunderbirds
and the wandering parade of Muscle Cars that stood tough

and proud, during the days when we forgot that we were here.
Praise to what stands in for us – when we fall from grace.

Praise to the painters, the scat graffiti artists, the lens keepers
and the sculptors that testify – through art – that we are here.

Praise to the echo of history and how its teleology is a wire –
connecting us and pulling us to what we are right here and now.

And pray – finally – that each new car will pilot us to our
farthest reach: that each divinity lane we drive on – I-94,

I-75, I-96, I-39 and The Lodge – will aim us all straight
through toward greater peace, toward indelible light, to grace.

The Archivists of the Incomprehensible

The archivists of the incomprehensible will one day
arrive here carrying their totems of change. Their bags of transcendence
and the ingredient eyeballs left over by startled partners going blind.

All the noise will be the commotion of an edible garden.
All the children will be laughing stomachs and merry go rounds.

All the women will be expansive ideas and glimmering lights.
All the men forecasts of heaven. All the streets ping pong.
All the birds aurora yellow stardust and vaudeville curtains.
The clowns will evaporate all the rubble. Fountains sing praise.

The story will be evolving. All the excess torn away like rain.
The future will be an envelope. The past a drug abuse recovery.
All the mementoes clutched in palms will be dancers leaping.

Busses will carry passengers into the hallways of a subversive love.
Work life will be a movie set where the ending owes the beginning.
Every person will be on the set and the arrangement will be ordinary.

The music will tell the archivists what will happen to grace.

What will happen to grace can't be predicted. Only the ordinary know.

The archivists of the incomprehensible are here now.

They shadow you while you shop at the farmer's market.
They align with you like the ghost in the abandoned vehicle.
They are the excess of the coming change. The forecast. The noise.
The magic box where death brings life. Life brings birth. The history
that's us.

The beautiful rust in the machine.

Watching De'Sean Jones at Bakers Keyboard Lounge

De'Sean Jones on the sax, blowing "Flow."
Maybe it's at Bakers, maybe just this ragged side
of the Davison Freeway, maybe at the pearly gates…

Does it get any cleaner than this? Does it get
any more muscular than what Detroit would ever ask for?

Any *more* committed to a just cause? Any greater?

Brother De'Sean, pulling the slinky, heavenly notes
out of the brass horn, drawing them up in a breath

and then pushing and propelling every one of them

out, just like clean clear light. Like a fountain's flow.

Leaning in close, to watch him blow, it seems to me
he's polishing a jazz saint's silver halo

all over this older plague of dissatisfied darkness.
He's just an alchemist, dusting off the gold.

He's a jazz *saint*, spreading, dotting, flecking the air clean.
We need him. Damn, we do.

The keyboardist's tickling the backside melody,

the drummer's splattering out a sidekick
of snare tricks, scatter-shot, slack-jawed, lazy, brisk,

and the trumpeter – he's hanging back,

polishing the song's greater burst and lather
with a smooth, brassy sass.

The rest of us, eager dwellers, lean forward.

Nothing stops De'Sean. He's after the spirit
of Detroit. His eyes squint, like he's

got the alien spirit of the future's greater flow,
right in sight.

Detroit River, January, 2020

I knelt at the Detroit River, my whole face ablaze
in rose-colored quartz as the winter morning sunlight,
spreading & stretching over the rippling waves,
surrendered itself like an expanding principality angel
offering me, & the day, a brand new coat of grace.
The Ambassador Bridge arched itself alive over water.
The buildings & the statues – lit up, spiritualized –
became fully incarnate, & the throngs of people
strolling to work – together, apart – were called to roll
& they marched as if they were of the city's 2nd
coming, its pulse. Detroit City, you elegance of cars
made of steel & the royal flush of musical prowess
& good luck, surround me with power: a power
that abolishes all this mean history we've weaponized
like a silver sword against all this great land we share;
all this possibility we hold together; all this storyline
that we hug & embrace so that I might now reveal
you as a liberty harbor, an altar, & a transfigured space
now fully imbued with good will & with light; with
holy grace & bold love, & a hereafter of good luck.

About the Author

Author photo: Keith Meisel

Ken Meisel is a poet from the Detroit area, a 2012 Kresge Arts Literary Fellow, and a Pushcart Prize nominee with publications in *Rattle, San Pedro River Review, Boxcar Review, Midwest Gothic* and *Pirene's Fountain*. His books include *Mortal Lullabies* (FutureCycle Press: 2018), *The Drunken Sweetheart at My Door* (FutureCycle Press: 2015), *Scrap Metal Mantra Poems* (Main Street Rag: 2013), and *Beautiful Rust* (Bottom Dog Press: 2009).

Made in the USA
Monee, IL
16 March 2020